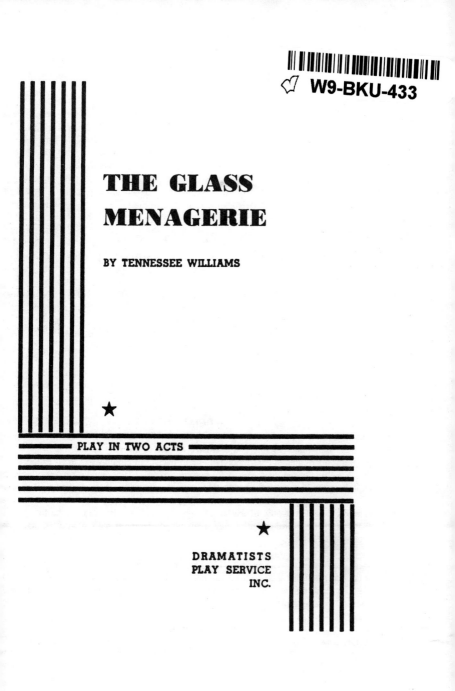

THE GLASS MENAGERIE

BY TENNESSEE WILLIAMS

★

PLAY IN TWO ACTS

★

DRAMATISTS
PLAY SERVICE
INC.

SPECIAL NOTE

Anyone receiving permission to produce THE GLASS MENAGERIE is required to give credit to the Author as sole and exclusive Author of the Play on the title page of all programs distributed in connection with performances of the Play and in all instances in which the title of the Play appears for purposes of advertising, publicizing or otherwise exploiting the Play and/or a production thereof. The name of the Author must appear on a separate line, in which no other name appears, immediately beneath the title and in size of type equal to 50% of the largest, most prominent letter used for the title of the Play. No person, firm or entity may receive credit larger or more prominent than that accorded the Author.

ALL TENNESSEE WILLIAMS PLAYS

It is understood that there will be no nudity in the Play unless specifically indicated in the script, and that nothing in the stage presentation or stage business in the Play will alter the spirit of the Play as written.

SPECIAL MUSIC TAPE

A tape containing the original music composed by Paul Bowles for the New York production of this play is available through the Play Service at *$20.00 per tape*, which includes packing and regular shipping. A cue sheet is included with the tape (cassette). *There is an additional royalty of $15.00 per performance* for the use of this music by producing groups.

Note on Incidental Music and Sound Effects

Music used in the original production of this play, composed by Paul Bowles, is available on a specially made cassette tape. This is sold on an outright basis, and includes all of Mr. Bowles' music written for the play. The use of this tape in the play requires a production fee, which is payable to the Service. The cassette may be ordered through the DRAMATISTS PLAY SERVICE at $20.00 per cassette, packing and regular shipping charges included.

The following is a list of sound effects referenced in this play:
Church bell
Thunder

As indicated in the text, victrola records used on-stage and dance music off-stage, are left to the discretion of the individual producer.

THE GLASS MENAGERIE was produced by Eddie Dowling and Louis J. Singer at the Playhouse Theatre, New York City, on March 31, 1945, with the following cast:

THE MOTHER............................Laurette Taylor

HER SON.................................Eddie Dowling

HER DAUGHTER...........................Julie Haydon

THE GENTLEMAN CALLER.................Anthony Ross

SCENE

An alley in St. Louis.

PART I: Preparation for a Gentleman Caller.

PART II: The Gentleman Calls.

TIME: Now and the Past.

Setting designed and lighted by Jo Mielziner.

Original Music composed by Paul Bowles.

Staged by Mr. Dowling and Margo Jones.

STAGING THE PLAY

Practical Suggestions by the Publisher

In issuing this new text of *The Glass Menagerie*, intended primarily for producing groups, a few words from us would seem called for. We urge all who are going to direct and mount the play to read these notes with care.

The present edition differs from the book of the play as first issued by Random House: the dialogue itself has to some extent been revised by the author, and the stage directions likewise. The latter have been drastically changed in order to guide the director and actor.

Mr. Williams' careful directions and explanations throughout the text will prove most helpful in that they crystallize and explain various moods which are to be sought, and while some of these directions are very specific, others are intended rather as guides to the creation of the necessary atmosphere. As the author has stated in his *Production Notes*, the play "can be presented with unusual freedom of convention."

The text printed in this book is a faithful indication of the way the play was produced in New York and on the road, but nonprofessional directors are advised to follow the actual means of presentation which seems to them most effective. In other words, such producers are offered any of a variety of different means of production, the only point to be stressed being that the production should of course adhere closely to the spirit of the play as written by the author.

For instance, the use of the two scrim curtains described in the stage directions may not be thought the best means of achieving that air of unreality that is often called for; the black-outs as described in the stage directions may be discarded for the occasional fall of the house curtain; Mr. Bowles' music (especially arranged on three records which we can furnish—see copyright page), although carefully cued into the text, need not necessarily be used at the precise places indicated by the music cues. It should be further stated that although the music on these records was that used for the professional production in New York, it is not absolutely essential that it should be used in this play at all. It is, however, highly recommended both by the author and by ourselves.

Special Note on Music Records: Some producers find it difficult to fit the music cues as indicated in this text into the three records. Bear in mind that the director is given almost complete leeway as to where the incidental music shall be used.

A few other points may be here indicated: the actual shape of the fire-escape landing may be modified; the alley-way at the left of the stage as indicated in the stage diagram, prepared especially for this acting edition by Mr. Jo Mielziner, on Page 63, need not (and probably will not) be used at all, and the one or two entrances mentioned as being made in that alley-way can very easily be made in the similar alley to the right of the stage; the music as played in the dance hall down right may be chosen from among the popular dance tunes of the 1920's, without reference to this or that particular title, while the same thing applies to the records used by Laura on the phonograph. While the exact position of each door and piece of furniture is described in the stage directions and shown in the stage diagram, the director should be permitted considerable leeway in making his own changes in such matters.

In a word, the present text gives all the hints, suggestions and actual directions for production, but provided the director, having studied what is here printed, wishes to use other means to achieve a complete and unified production according to his own views, he should be encouraged to do so.

It should certainly be made clear to most directors that too great concern over certain technical details is not only unnecessary, but may easily interfere with the totality of effect to be sought throughout the entire play. For example, the glass figures which are Laura's "menagerie" need be no more than small clear glass objects which can be barely distinguished by the audience, presumably a few small cheap ornaments that can be bought at any ten-cent store.

The only off-stage sound effects of any complexity or importance are the thunder and distant church bells as described in the stage directions. Sound effect records suggesting these are mentioned on the copyright page of the present volume.

DRAMATISTS PLAY SERVICE, INC.

AUTHOR'S PRODUCTION NOTES

Being a "memory play," *The Glass Menagerie* can be presented with unusual freedom of convention. Because of its considerably delicate or tenuous material, atmospheric touches and subtleties of direction play a particularly important part. Expressionism and all other unconventional techniques in drama have only one valid aim, and that is a closer approach to truth. When a play employs unconventional techniques, it is not, or certainly shouldn't be, trying to escape its responsibility of dealing with reality, or interpreting experience, but is actually or should be attempting to find a closer approach, a more penetrating and vivid expression of things as they are. The straight realistic play with its genuine frigidaire and authentic ice-cubes, its characters that speak exactly as its audience speaks, corresponds to the academic landscape and has the same virtue of a photographic likeness. Everyone should know nowadays the unimportance of the photographic in art: that truth, life, or reality is an organic thing which the poetic imagination can represent or suggest, in essence, only through transformation, through changing into other forms than those which were merely present in appearance.

These remarks are not meant as a preface only to this particular play. They have to do with a conception of a new, plastic theatre which must take the place of the exhausted theatre of realistic conventions if the theatre is to resume vitality as a part of our culture.

The Music

Another extra-literary accent in this play is provided by the use of music. A single recurring tune, "The Glass Menagerie," is used to give emotional emphasis to suitable passages. This tune is like circus music, not when you are on the grounds or in the immediate vicinity of the parade, but when you are at some distance and very likely thinking of something else. It seems under those circumstances to continue almost interminably and it weaves in and out of your preoccupied consciousness; then it is the lightest, most delicate music in the world and perhaps the saddest. It expresses the surface vivacity of life with the underlying strain of immutable and inexpressible sorrow. When you look at a piece of delicately spun glass you think of two things: how beautiful it is and how easily it can be broken. Both of those ideas should be woven into the recurring tune, which dips in and out of the play as if it were carried on a wind that changes. It serves as a thread of connection and allusion between the narrator with his separate point

7

in time and space and the subject of his story. Between each episode it returns as reference to the emotion, nostalgia, which is the first condition of the play. It is primarily Laura's music and therefore comes out most clearly when the play focuses upon her and the lovely fragility of glass which is her image.

THE LIGHTING

The lighting in the play is not realistic. In keeping with the atmosphere of memory, the stage is dim. Shafts of light are focused on selected areas or actors, sometimes in contradistinction to what is the apparent center. For instance, in the quarrel scene between Tom and Amanda, in which Laura has no active part, the clearest pool of light is on her figure. This is also true of the supper scene, when her silent figure on the sofa should remain the visual center. The light upon Laura should be distinct from the others, having a peculiar pristine clarity such as light used in early religious portraits of female saints or madonnas. A certain correspondence to light in religious paintings, such as El Greco's, where the figures are radiant in atmosphere that is relatively dusky, could be effectively used throughout the play. (It will also permit a more effective use of the screen.) A free, imaginative use of light can be of enormous value in giving a mobile, plastic quality to plays of a more or less static nature.

NOTES ON THE CHARACTERS

AMANDA WINGFIELD (the mother): A little woman of great but confused vitality, clinging frantically to another time and place. Her characterization must be carefully created, not copied from type. She is not paranoiac, but her life is paranoia. There is much to admire in Amanda, and as much to love and pity as there is to laugh at. Certainly she has endurance and a kind of heroism, and though her foolishness makes her unwittingly cruel at times, there is tenderness in her slight person.

LAURA WINGFIELD (her daughter): Amanda, having failed to establish contact with reality, continues to live vitally in her illusions, but Laura's situation is even graver. A childhood illness has left her crippled, one leg slightly shorter than the other, and held in a brace. This defect need not be more than suggested on the stage. Stemming from this, Laura's separation increases till she is like a piece of her own glass collection, too exquisitely fragile to move from the shelf.

TOM WINGFIELD (her son): And the narrator of the play. A poet with a job in a warehouse. His nature is not remorseless, but to escape from a trap he has to act without pity.

JIM O'CONNOR (the gentleman caller): A nice, ordinary, young man.

T. W.

THE GLASS MENAGERIE

ACT I

SCENE 1

The Wingfield apartment is in the rear of the building, one of those vast hive-like conglomerations of cellular living-units that flower as warty growths in over-crowded urban centers of lower middle-class population and are symptomatic of the impulse of this largest and fundamentally enslaved section of American society to avoid fluidity and differentiation and to exist and function as one interfused mass of automatism. The apartment faces an alley and is entered by a fire-escape, a structure whose name is a touch of accidental poetic truth, for all of these huge buildings are always burning with the slow and implacable fires of human desperation. The fire-escape is included in the set—that is, the landing of it and steps descending from it. (Note that the stage L. alley may be entirely omitted, since it is never used except for Tom's first entrance, which can take place stage R.) The scene is memory and is therefore nonrealistic. Memory takes a lot of poetic license. It omits some details, others are exaggerated, according to the emotional value of the articles it touches, for memory is seated predominantly in the heart. The interior is therefore rather dim and poetic. (CUE #1. As soon as the house lights dim, dance-hall music heard on-stage R. Old popular music of, say, 1915-1920 period. This continues until Tom is at fire-escape landing, having lighted cigarette, and begins speaking.)
AT RISE: *At the rise of the house curtain, the audience is faced with the dark, grim rear wall of the Wingfield tenement. (The stage set proper is screened out by a gauze curtain, which suggests the front part, outside, of the building.) This building, which runs parallel to the footlights, is flanked on both sides by dark, narrow alleys*

9

which run into murky canyons of tangled clotheslines, garbage cans and the sinister lattice-work of neighboring fire-escapes. (The alleys are actually in darkness, and the objects just mentioned are not visible.) It is up and down these side alleys that exterior entrances and exits are made, during the play. At the end of Tom's opening commentary, the dark tenement wall slowly reveals (by means of a transparency) the interior of the ground floor Wingfield apartment. (Gauze curtain, which suggests front part of building, rises on the interior set.) Downstage is the living room, which also serves as a sleeping room for Laura, the day-bed unfolding to make her bed. Just above this is a small stool or table on which is a telephone. Upstage, C., and divided by a wide arch or second proscenium with transparent faded portieres (or second curtain; "second curtain" is actually the inner gauze curtain between the living-room and the dining-room, which is upstage of it), is the dining-room. In an old-fashioned what-not in the living-room are seen scores of transparent glass animals. A blown-up photograph of the father hangs on the wall of the living-room, facing the audience, to the L. of the archway. It is the face of a very handsome young man in a doughboy's First World War cap. He is gallantly smiling, ineluctably smiling, as if to say, "I will be smiling forever." (Note that all that is essential in connection with dance-hall is that the window be shown lighting lower part of alley. It is not necessary to show any considerable part of dance-hall.) The audience hears and sees the opening scene in the dining-room through both the transparent fourth wall (this is the gauze curtain which suggests outside of building) of the building and the transparent gauze portieres of the dining-room arch. It is during this revealing scene that the fourth wall slowly ascends, out of sight. This transparent exterior wall is not brought down again until the very end of the play, during Tom's final speech. The narrator is an undisguised convention of the play. He takes whatever license with dramatic convention as is convenient to his purposes.

Tom enters dressed as a merchant sailor from alley, stage L. (i.e., stage R. if L. alley is omitted), and strolls across *the front of the stage to the fire-escape. (This is the fire-escape landing shown in diagram on p. 69. Tom may lean against grillwork of this as he lights cigarette.) There he stops and lights a cigarette. He addresses the audience.*

TOM. I have tricks in my pocket—I have things up my sleeve— but I am the opposite of the stage magician. He gives you illusion that has the appearance of truth. I give you truth in the pleasant disguise of illusion. I take you back to an alley in St. Louis. The time that quaint period when the huge middle class of America was matriculating from a school for the blind. Their eyes had failed them, or they had failed their eyes, and so they were having their fingers pressed forcibly down on the fiery Braille alphabet of a dissolving economy.—In Spain there was revolution.—Here there was only shouting and confusion and labor disturbances, some- times violent, in otherwise peaceful cities such as Cleveland— Chicago—Detroit. . . . That is the social background of this play . . . The play is memory. (MUSIC CUE #2) Being a memory play, it is dimly lighted, it is sentimental, it is not realistic.—In memory everything seems to happen to music.—That explains the fiddle in the wings. I am the narrator of the play, and also a char- acter in it. The others characters in the play are my mother, Amanda, my sister, Laura, and a gentleman caller who appears in the final scenes. He is the most realistic character in the play, be- ing an emissary from a world that we were somehow set apart from.—But having a poet's weakness for symbols, I am using this character as a symbol—as the long-delayed but always expected something that we live for.—There is a fifth character who doesn't appear other than in a photograph hanging on the wall. When you see the picture of this grinning gentleman, please remember this is our father who left us a long time ago. He was a telephone man who fell in love with long distance—so he gave up his job with the telephone company and skipped the light fantastic out of town. . . . The last we heard of him was a picture postcard from the Pacific coast of Mexico, containing a message of two words— "Hello—Good-bye!" and no address. (LIGHTS UP IN DINING ROOM. *Tom exits* R. *He goes off downstage, takes off his sailor overcoat and skull-fitting knitted cap and remains off-stage by din- ing-room* R. *door for his entrance cue. Amanda's voice becomes audible through the portieres—i.e., gauze curtains separating din-*

11

ing-room from living-room. Amanda and Laura are seated at a drop-leaf table. Amanda is sitting in C. chair and Laura in L. chair. Eating is indicated by gestures without food or utensils. Amanda faces the audience. The interior of the dining-room has lit up softly and through the scrim—gauze curtains—we see Amanda and Laura seated at the table in the upstage area.)

AMANDA. You know, Laura, I had the funniest experience in church last Sunday. The church was crowded except for one pew way down front and in that was just one little woman. I smiled very sweetly at her and said, "Excuse me, would you mind if I shared this pew?" "I certainly would," she said, "this space is rented." Do you know that is the first time that I ever knew that the Lord rented space. *(Dining-room gauze curtains open automatically.)* These Northern Episcopalians! I can understand the Southern Episcopalians, but these Northern ones, no. *(Tom enters dining-room R., slips over to table and sits in chair R.)* Honey, don't push your food with your fingers. If you have to push your food with something, the thing to use is a crust of bread. You must chew your food. Animals have secretions in their stomachs which enable them to digest their food without mastication, but human beings must chew their food before they swallow it down, and chew, chew. Oh, eat leisurely. Eat leisurely. A well-cooked meal has many delicate flavors that have to be held in the mouth for appreciation, not just gulped down. Oh, chew, chew—chew! *(At this point the scrim curtain—if the director decides to use it—the one suggesting exterior wall, rises here and does not come down again until just before the end of the play.)* Don't you want to give your salivary glands a chance to function?

TOM. Mother, I haven't enjoyed one bite of my dinner because of your constant directions on how to eat it. It's you that makes me hurry through my meals with your hawk-like attention to every bite I take. It's disgusting—all this discussion of animals' secretion —salivary glands—mastication! *(Comes down to arm-chair in living room R., lights cigarette.)*

AMANDA. Temperament like a Metropolitan star! You're not excused from this table.

TOM. I'm getting a cigarette.

AMANDA. You smoke too much.

LAURA. *(Rising.)* Mother, I'll bring in the coffee.

AMANDA. No, no, no, no. You sit down. I'm going to be the colored boy today and you're going to be the lady.

LAURA. I'm already up.

AMANDA. Resume your seat. Resume your seat. You keep yourself fresh and pretty for the gentlemen callers. (*Laura sits.*)

LAURA. I'm not expecting any gentlemen callers.

AMANDA. (*Who has been gathering dishes from table and loading them on tray.*) Well, the nice thing about them is they come when they're least expected. Why, I remember one Sunday afternoon in Blue Mountain when your mother was a girl . . . (*Goes out for coffee, U. R.*)

TOM. I know what's coming now! (*Laura rises.*)

LAURA. Yes. But let her tell it. (*Crosses to L. of day-bed, sits.*)

TOM. Again?

LAURA. She loves to tell it.

AMANDA. (*Entering from R. in dining-room and coming down into living-room with tray and coffee.*) I remember one Sunday afternoon in Blue Mountain when your mother was a girl she received—seventeen—gentlemen callers! (*Amanda crosses to Tom at armchair R., gives him coffee, and crosses C. Laura comes to her, takes cup, resumes her place on L. of day-bed. Amanda puts tray on small table R. of day-bed, sits R. on day-bed. Inner curtain closes, light dims out.*) Why, sometimes there weren't chairs enough to accommodate them all and we had to send the colored boy over to the parish house to fetch the folding chairs.

TOM. How did you entertain all those gentlemen callers? (*Tom finally sits in armchair R.*)

AMANDA. I happened to understand the art of conversation!

TOM. I bet you could talk!

AMANDA. Well, I could. All the girls in my day could, I tell you.

TOM. Yes?

AMANDA. They knew how to entertain their gentlemen callers. It wasn't enough for a girl to be possessed of a pretty face and a graceful figure—although I wasn't slighted in either respect. She also needed to have a nimble wit and a tongue to meet all occasions.

TOM. What did you talk about?

AMANDA. Why, we'd talk about things of importance going on in the world! Never anything common or coarse or vulgar. My callers were gentlemen—all! Some of the most prominent men on

13

the Mississippi Delta—planters and sons of planters! There was young Champ Laughlin. (MUSIC CUE #3.) He later became Vice-President of the Delta Planters' Bank. And Hadley Stevenson; he was drowned in Moon Lake.—My goodness, he certainly left his widow well provided for—a hundred and fifty thousand dollars in government bonds. And the Cutrere Brothers—Wesley and Bates. Bates was one of my own bright particular beaus! But he got in a quarrel with that wild Wainwright boy and they shot it out on the floor of Moon Lake Casino. Bates was shot through the stomach. He died in the ambulance on his way to Memphis. He certainly left his widow well provided for, too—eight or ten thousand acres, no less. He never loved that woman; she just caught him on the rebound. My picture was found on him the night he died. Oh and that boy, that boy that every girl in the Delta was setting her cap for! That beautiful (MUSIC FADES OUT) brilliant young Fitzhugh boy from Greene County!

TOM. What did he leave his widow?

AMANDA. He never married! What's the matter with you—you talk as though all my old admirers had turned up their toes to the daisies!

TOM. Isn't this the first you've mentioned that still survives?

AMANDA. He made an awful lot of money. He went North to Wall Street and made a fortune. He had the Midas touch—everything that boy touched just turned to gold! (*Gets up.*) And I could have been Mrs. J. Duncan Fitzhugh—mind you! (*Crosses* L. C.) But—what did I do?—I just went out of my way and picked your father! (*Looks at picture on* L. *wall. Goes to small table* R. *of day-bed for tray.*)

LAURA. (*Rises from day-bed.*) Mother, let me clear the table.

AMANDA. (*Crossing* L. *for Laura's cup, then crossing* R. *for Tom's.*) No, dear, you go in front and study your typewriter chart.` Or practice your shorthand a little. Stay fresh and pretty! It's almost time for our gentlemen callers to start arriving. How many do you suppose we're going to entertain this afternoon? (*Tom opens curtains between dining-room and living-room for her. These close behind her, and she exits into kitchen* R. *Tom stands* U. C. *in living-room.*)

LAURA. (*To Amanda, off-stage.*) I don't believe we're going to receive any, Mother.

AMANDA. (*Off-stage.*) Not any? Not one? Why, you must be

14

joking! Not one gentleman caller? What's the matter? Has there been a flood or a tornado?

LAURA. (*Crossing to typing table.*) It isn't a flood. It's not a tornado, Mother. I'm just not popular like you were in Blue Mountain. Mother's afraid that I'm going to be an old maid. (MUSIC CUE #4.) (*Lights dim out. Tom exits* U. C. *in blackout. Laura crosses to menagerie* R.)

ACT I

SCENE 2

Scene is the same. Lights dim up on living-room.
Laura discovered by menagerie, polishing glass. Crosses to phonograph, play record.[1] She times this business so as to put needle on record as MUSIC CUE #4 ends. Enter Amanda down alley R. *Rattles key in lock. Laura crosses guiltily to typewriter and types. (Small typewriter table with typewriter on it is still on stage in living-room* L.) *Amanda comes into room* R. *closing door. Crosses to armchair, putting hat, purse and gloves on it. Something has happened to Amanda. It is written in her face: a look that is grim and hopeless and a little absurd. She has on one of those cheap or imitation velvety-looking cloth coats with imitation fur collar. Her hat is five or six years old, one of those dreadful cloche hats that were worn in the late twenties and she is clasping an enormous black patent-leather pocketbook with nickel clasps and initials. This is her full-dress outfit, the one she usually wears to the D.A.R. She purses her lips, opens her eyes very wide, rolls them upward and shakes her head. Seeing her mother's expression, Laura touches her lips with a nervous gesture.*

LAURA. Hello, Mother, I was just . . .
AMANDA. I know. You were just practicing your typing, I suppose. (*Behind chair* R.)

[1] While *Dardanella* was used in the professional production, any other popular record of the 20's may be substituted. It should be a worn record.

15

LAURA. Yes.

AMANDA. Deception, deception, deception!

LAURA. (*Shakily.*) How was the D.A.R. meeting, Mother?

AMANDA. (*Crosses to Laura.*) D.A.R. meeting!

LAURA. Didn't you go to the D.A.R. meeting, Mother?

AMANDA. (*Faintly, almost inaudibly.*) No, I didn't go to any D.A.R. meeting. (*Then more forcibly.*) I didn't have the strength —I didn't have the courage. I just wanted to find a hole in the ground and crawl in it and stay there the rest of my entire life. (*Tears type charts, throws them on floor.*)

LAURA. (*Faintly.*) Why did you do that, Mother?

AMANDA. (*Sits on* R. *end of day-bed.*) Why? Why? How old are you, Laura?

LAURA. Mother, you know my age.

AMANDA. I was under the impression that you were an adult, but evidently I was very much mistaken. (*She stares at Laura.*)

LAURA. Please don't stare at me, Mother! (*Amanda closes her eyes and lowers her head. Pause.*)

AMANDA. What are we going to do? What is going to become of us? What is the future? (*Pause.*)

LAURA. Has something happened, Mother? Mother, has something happened?

AMANDA. I'll be all right in a minute. I'm just bewildered—by life . . .

LAURA. Mother, I wish that you would tell me what's happened!

AMANDA. I went to the D.A.R. this afternoon, as you know; I was to be inducted as an officer. I stopped off at Rubicam's Business College to tell them about your cold and to ask how you were progressing down there.

LAURA. Oh . . .

AMANDA. Yes, oh—oh—oh. I went straight to your typing instructor and introduced myself as your mother. She didn't even know who you were. Wingfield, she said? We don't have any such scholar enrolled in this school. I assured her she did. I said my daughter Laura's been coming to classes since early January. "Well, I don't know," she said, "unless you mean that terribly shy little girl who dropped out of school after a few days' attendance?" No, I said, I don't mean that one. I mean my daughter, Laura, who's been coming here every single day for the past six weeks! "Excuse me," she said. And she took down the attendance book and there was your name, unmistakable, printed, and all the dates you'd been absent. I still told her she was wrong. I still said, "No, there must have been some mistake! There must have been some mix-up in the records!" "No," she said, "I remember her perfectly now. She was so shy and her hands trembled so that her fingers couldn't touch the right keys! When we gave a speed-test—she just broke down completely—was sick at the stomach and had to be carried to the washroom! After that she never came back. We telephoned the house every single day and never got any answer." (*Rises from day-bed, crosses* R. C.) That was while I was working all day long down at that department store, I suppose, demonstrating those —— (*With hands indicates brassiere.*) Oh! I felt so weak I couldn't stand up! (*Sits in armchair.*) I had to sit down while they got me a glass of water! (*Laura crosses up to phonograph.*) Fifty dollars' tuition. I don't care about the money so much, but all my hopes for any kind of future for you—gone up the spout, just gone up the spout like that. (*Laura winds phonograph up.*) Oh, don't *do* that, Laura!—Don't play that victrola!

LAURA. Oh! (*Stops phonograph, crosses to typing table, sits.*)

AMANDA. What have you been doing every day when you've gone out of the house pretending that you were going to business college?

LAURA. I've just been going out walking.

AMANDA. That's not true!

LAURA. Yes, it is, Mother, I just went walking.

AMANDA. Walking? Walking? In winter? Deliberately courting pneumonia in that light coat? Where did you walk to, Laura?

LAURA. All sorts of places—mostly in the park.

AMANDA. Even after you'd started catching that cold?

LAURA. It was the lesser of two evils, Mother. I couldn't go back. I threw up on the floor!

AMANDA. From half-past seven till after five every day you mean to tell me you walked around in the park, because you wanted to make me think that you were still going to Rubicam's Business College?

LAURA. Oh, Mother, it wasn't as bad as it sounds. I went inside places to get warmed up.

AMANDA. Inside where?

LAURA. I went in the art museum and the bird-houses at the Zoo.

17

I visited the penguins every day! Sometimes I did without lunch and went to the movies. Lately I've been spending most of my afternoons in the Jewel-box, that big glass house where they raise the tropical flowers.

AMANDA. You did all that to deceive me, just for deception! Why? Why? Why? Why?

LAURA. Mother, when you're disappointed, you get that awful suffering look on your face, like the picture of Jesus' mother in the Museum! (*Rises.*)

AMANDA. Hush!

LAURA. (*Crosses* R. *to menagerie.*) I couldn't face it. I couldn't. (MUSIC CUE #5.)

AMANDA. (*Rising from day-bed.*) So what are we going to do now, honey, the rest of our lives? Just sit down in this house and watch the parades go by? Amuse ourselves with the glass menagerie? Eternally play those worn-out records your father left us as a painful reminder of him? (*Slams phonograph lid.*) We can't have a business career. (END MUSIC CUE #5.) No, we can't do that—that just gives us indigestion. (*Around* R. *day-bed.*) What is there left for us now but dependency all our lives? I tell you, Laura, I know so well what happens to unmarried women who aren't prepared to occupy a position in life. (*Crosses* L., *sits on day-bed.*) I've seen such pitiful cases in the South—barely tolerated spinsters living on some brother's wife or a sister's husband—tucked away in some mouse-trap of a room—encouraged by one in-law to go on and visit the next in-law—little birdlike women—without any nest—eating the crust of humility all their lives! Is that the future that we've mapped out for ourselves? I swear I don't see any other alternative. And I don't think that's a very pleasant alternative. Of course—some girls *do* marry. My goodness, Laura, haven't you ever liked some boy?

LAURA. Yes, Mother, I liked one once.

AMANDA. You did?

LAURA. I came across his picture a while ago.

AMANDA. He gave you his picture, too? (*Rises from day-bed, crosses to chair* R.)

LAURA. No, it's in the year-book.

AMANDA. (*Sits in armchair.*) Oh—a high-school boy.

LAURA. Yes. His name was Jim. (*Kneeling on floor, gets year-*

18

book from under menagerie.) Here he is in "The Pirates of Pen-zance."

AMANDA. (*Absently.*) The what?

LAURA. The operetta the senior class put on. He had a wonderful voice. We sat across the aisle from each other Mondays, Wednes-days and Fridays in the auditorium. Here he is with a silver cup for debating! See his grin?

AMANDA. So he had a grin, too! (*Looks at picture of father on wall behind phonograph.[2] Hands year-book back.*)

LAURA. He used to call me—Blue Roses.

AMANDA. Blue Roses? What did he call you a silly name like that for?

LAURA. (*Still kneeling.*) When I had that attack of pleurosis—he asked me what was the matter when I came back. I said pleurosis—he thought that I said "Blue Roses." So that's what he always called me after that. Whenever he saw me, he'd holler, "Hello, Blue Roses!" I didn't care for the girl that he went out with. Emily Meisenbach. Oh, Emily was the best-dressed girl at Soldan. But she never struck me as being sincere . . . I read in a newspaper once that they were engaged. (*Puts year-book back on a shelf of glass menagerie.*) That's a long time ago—they're probably married by now.

AMANDA. That's all right, honey, that's all right. It doesn't mat-ter. Little girls who aren't cut out for business careers sometimes end up married to very nice young men. And I'm just going to see that you do that, too!

LAURA. But, Mother ——

AMANDA. What is it now?

LAURA. I'm—crippled!

AMANDA. Don't say that word! (*Rises, crosses to C. Turns to Laura.*) How many times have I told you never to say that word! You're not crippled, you've just got a slight defect. (*Laura rises.*) If you lived in the days when I was a girl and they had long graceful skirts sweeping the ground, it might have been considered an asset. When you've got a slight disadvantage like that, you've just got to cultivate something else to take its place. You have to

2 In the original production this photo was a life-sized head. It lights up from time to time as indicated. The illumination may, if desired, be omitted. If used, it lights here.

19

cultivate charm—or vivacity—or *charm!* (*Spotlight on photograph.*[3] *Then dim out.*) That's the only thing your father had plenty of—charm! (*Amanda sits on day-bed. Laura crosses to arm-chair and sits.*) (MUSIC CUE #6.) (*Blackout.*)

ACT I

SCENE 3

SCENE: *The same. Lights up again but only on* R. *alley and fire-escape landing, rest of the stage dark.* (*Type-writer table and typewriter have been taken off-stage.*) *Enter Tom, again wearing merchant sailor overcoat and knitted cap, in alley* R. *As* MUSIC CUE #6 *ends, Tom begins to speak.*

TOM. (*Leans against grill of fire-escape, smoking.*) After the fiasco at Rubicam's Business College, the idea of getting a gentleman caller for my sister Laura began to play a more and more important part in my mother's calculations. It became an obsession. Like some archetype of the universal unconscious, the image of the gentleman caller haunted our small apartment. An evening at home rarely passed without some allusion to this image, this spectre, this hope. . . . And even when he wasn't mentioned, his presence hung in my mother's preoccupied look and in my sister's frightened, apologetic manner. It hung like a sentence passed upon the Wingfields! But my mother was a woman of action as well as words. (MUSIC CUE #7.) She began to take logical steps in the planned direction. Late that winter and in the early spring—realizing that extra money would be needed to properly feather the nest and plume the bird—she began a vigorous campaign on the telephone, roping in subscribers to one of those magazines for matrons called "The Homemaker's Companion," the type of journal that features the serialized sublimations of ladies of letters who think in terms of delicate cup-like breasts, slim, tapering waists, rich creamy thighs, eyes like wood-smoke in autumn, fingers that soothe and caress like soft, soft strains of music. Bodies as powerful as Etruscan sculpture. (*He exits down* R. *into wings. Light in alley* R. *is*

[3] See note on page 19.

20

blacked out, and a head-spot falls on Amanda, at phone in living-room. MUSIC CUE #7 ends as Tom stops speaking.)

AMANDA. Ida Scott? *(During this speech Tom enters dining-room* u. r. *unseen by audience, not wearing overcoat or hat. There is an unlighted reading lamp on table. Sits* c. *of dining-room table with writing materials.)* This is Amanda Wingfield. We missed you at the D.A.R. last Monday. Oh, first I want to know how's your sinus condition? You're just a Christian martyr. That's what you are. You're just a Christian martyr. Well, I was just going through my little red book, and I saw that your subscription to the "Companion" is about to expire just when that wonderful new serial by Bessie Mae Harper is starting. It's the first thing she's written since "Honeymoon for Three." Now, that was unusual, wasn't it? Why, Ida, this one is even lovelier. It's all about the horsey set on Long Island and a debutante is thrown from her horse while taking him over the jumps at the—regatta. Her spine—her spine is injured. That's what the horse did—he stepped on her. Now, there is only one surgeon in the entire world that can keep her from being completely paralyzed, and that's the man she's engaged to be married to and he's tall and he's blond and he's handsome. That's unusual, too, huh? Oh, he's not perfect. Of course he has a weakness. He has the most terrible weakness in the entire world. He just drinks too much. What? Oh, no, Honey, don't let them burn. You go take a look in the oven and I'll hold on . . . Why, that woman! Do you know what she did? She hung up on me. *(Dining-room and living-room lights dim in. Reading lamp lights up at same time.)*

LAURA. Oh, Mother, Mother, Tom's trying to write. *(Rises from armchair where she was left at curtain of previous scene, goes to curtain between dining-room and living-room, which is already open.)*

AMANDA. Oh! So he is. So he is. *(Crosses from phone, goes to dining-room and up to Tom.)*

TOM. *(At table.)* Now what are you up to?

AMANDA. I'm trying to save your eyesight. *(Business with lamp.)* You've only got one pair of eyes and you've got to take care of them. Oh, I know that Milton was blind, but that's not what made him a genius.

TOM. Mother, will you please go away and let me finish my writing?

21

AMANDA. (*Squares his shoulders.*) Why can't you sit up straight? So your shoulders don't stick through like sparrows' wings?

TOM. Mother, please go busy yourself with something else. I'm trying to write.

AMANDA. (*Business with Tom.*) Now, I've seen a medical chart, and I know what that position does to your internal organs. You sit up and I'll show you. Your stomach presses against your lungs, and your lungs press against your heart, and that poor little heart gets discouraged because it hasn't got any room left to go on beating for you.

TOM. What in hell . . . ! (*Inner curtains between living-room and dining-room close. Lights dim down in dining-room. Laura crosses, stands C. of curtains in living-room listening to following scene between Tom and Amanda.*)

AMANDA.[4] Don't you talk to me like that ——

TOM. —am I supposed to do?

AMANDA. What's the matter with you? Have you gone out of your senses?

TOM. Yes, I have. You've driven me out of them.

AMANDA. What is the matter with you lately, you big—big—idiot?

TOM. Look, Mother—I haven't got a thing, not a single thing left in this house that I can call my own.

AMANDA. Lower your voice!

TOM. Yesterday you confiscated my books! You had the nerve to ——

AMANDA. I did. I took that horrible novel back to the library —that awful book by that insane Mr. Lawrence. I cannot control the output of a diseased mind or people who cater to them, but I won't allow such filth in my house. No, no, no, no, no!

TOM. House, house! Who pays the rent on the house, who makes a slave of himself to ——!

AMANDA. Don't you dare talk to me like that! (*Laura crosses D. L. to back of armchair.*)

TOM. No, I mustn't say anything! I've just got to keep quiet and let you do all the talking.

AMANDA. Let me tell you something!

TOM. I don't want to hear any more.

4 Tom and Amanda remain in dining-room throughout their argument.

22

AMANDA. You will hear more —— (*Laura crosses to phonograph.*)

TOM. (*Crossing through curtains between dining-room and living-room. Goes up stage of door* R. *where, in a dark spot, there is supposedly a closet.*) Well, I'm not going to listen. I'm going out. (*Gets out coat.*)

AMANDA. (*Coming through curtains into living-room, stands* C.) You are going to listen to me, Tom Wingfield. I'm tired of your impudence.—And another thing—I'm right at the end of my patience!

TOM. (*Putting overcoat on back of armchair and crossing back to Amanda.*) What do you think I'm at the end of, Mother? Aren't I supposed to have any patience to reach the end of? I know, I know. It seems unimportant, to you, what I'm *doing*—what I'm trying to do—having a difference between them! You don't think that.

AMANDA. I think you're doing things that you're ashamed of, and that's why you act like this. (*Tom crosses to day-bed and sits.*) I don't believe that you go every night to the movies. Nobody goes to the movies night after night. Nobody in their right minds goes to the movies as often as you pretend to. People don't go to the movies at nearly midnight and movies don't let out at two A.M. Come in stumbling, muttering to yourself like a maniac. You get three hours' sleep and then go to work. Oh, I can picture the way you're doing down there. Moping, doping, because you're in no condition.

TOM. That's true—that's very, very true. I'm in no condition!

AMANDA. How dare you jeopardize your job? Jeopardize our security? How do you think we'd manage ——? (*Sits armchair* R.)

TOM. Look, Mother, do you think I'm crazy about the *warehouse?* You think I'm in love with the Continental Shoemakers? You think I want to spend fifty-five years of my life down there in that—*celotex interior!* with *fluorescent tubes?!* Honest to God, I'd rather somebody picked up a crow-bar and battered out my brains—than go back mornings! But I *go!* Sure, every time you come in yelling that bloody *Rise and Shine! Rise and shine!!* I think how lucky dead people are! But I get up. (*Rises from day-bed.*) I *go!* For sixty-five dollars a month I give up all that I dream of

23

doing and being *ever!* And you say that is all I think of. Oh, God! Why, Mother, if self is all I ever thought of, Mother, *I'd be where he is—GONE!* (*Crosses to get overcoat on back of armchair.*) As far as the system of transportation reaches! (*Amanda rises, crosses to him and grabs his arm.*) Please don't grab at me, Mother!

AMANDA. (*Following him.*) I'm not grabbing at you. I want to know where you're going now.

TOM. (*Taking overcoat and starts crossing to door* R.) I'm going to the movies!

AMANDA. (*Crosses* C.) I don't believe that lie!

TOM. (*Crosses back to Amanda.*) No? Well, you're right. For once in your life you're right. I'm not going to the movies. I'm going to opium dens! Yes, Mother, opium dens, dens of vice and criminals' hang-outs, Mother. I've joined the Hogan gang. I'm a hired assassin, I carry a tommy-gun in a violin case! I run a string of cathouses in the valley! They call me Killer, Killer Wingfield, I'm really leading a double life. By day I'm a simple, honest warehouse worker, but at night I'm a dynamic czar of the underworld. Why, I go to gambling casinos and spin away a fortune on the roulette table! I wear a patch over one eye and a false moustache, sometimes I wear green whiskers. On those occasions they call me— El Diablo! Oh, I could tell you things to make you sleepless! My enemies plan to dynamite this place some night! Some night they're going to blow us all sky-high. And will I be glad! Will I be happy! And so will you be. You'll go up—up—over Blue Mountain on a broomstick! With seventeen gentlemen callers! You ugly babbling old witch! (*He goes through a series of violent, clumsy movements, seizing his overcoat, lunging to* R. *door, pulling it fiercely open. The women watch him, aghast. His arm catches in the sleeve of the coat as he struggles to pull it on. For a moment he is pinioned by the bulky garment. With an outraged groan he tears the coat off again, splitting the shoulder of it, and hurls it across the room. It strikes against the shelf of Laura's glass collection, there is a tinkle of shattering glass. Laura cries out as if wounded.*)

LAURA. My glass!—menagerie . . . (*She covers her face and turns away.* MUSIC CUE #8 *through to end of scene.*)

AMANDA. (*In an awful voice.*) I'll never speak to you again as long as you live unless you apologize to me! (*Amanda exits through living-room curtains. Tom is left with Laura. He stares at*

24

her stupidly for a moment. Then he crosses to shelf holding glass menagerie. Drops awkwardly on his knees to collect fallen glass, glancing at Laura as if he would speak, but couldn't. Blackout. Tom, Amanda and Laura exit in blackout.)

ACT I

Scene 4

The interior is dark. Faint light in alley R. A deep-voiced bell in a church is tolling the hour of five as the scene commences.

Tom appears at the top of R. alley. After each solemn boom of the bell in the tower he shakes a little toy noise-maker or rattle as if to express the tiny spasm of man in contrast to the sustained power and dignity of the Almighty. This and the unsteadiness of his advance make it evident that he has been drinking. As he climbs the few steps to the fire-escape landing light steals up inside. Laura appears in night-dress, entering living-room from L. door of dining-room, observing Tom's empty bed (day-bed) in the living-room. Tom fishes in his pockets for door-key, removing a motley assortment of articles in the search, including a perfect shower of movie-ticket stubs and an empty bottle. At last he finds the key, but just as he is about to insert it, it slips from his fingers. He strikes a match and crouches below the door.

TOM. (Bitterly.) One crack—and it falls through! (*Laura opens door R.*) [5]
LAURA. Tom! Tom, what are you doing?
TOM. Looking for a door-key.
LAURA. Where have you been all this time?
TOM. I have been to the movies.
LAURA. All this time at the movies?
TOM. There was a very long program. There was a Garbo picture and a Mickey Mouse and a travelogue and a newsreel and a pre-view of coming attractions. And there was an organ solo and a

[5] Next few speeches are spoken on fire-escape landing.

collection for the milk-fund—simultaneously—which ended up in a terrible fight between a fat lady and an usher!

LAURA. (*Innocently.*) Did you have to stay through everything?

TOM. Of course! And, oh, I forgot! There was a big stage show! The headliner on this stage show was Malvolio the Magician. He performed wonderful tricks, many of them, such as pouring water back and forth between pitchers. First it turned to wine and then it turned to beer and then it turned to whiskey. I know it was whiskey it finally turned into because he needed somebody to come up out of the audience to help him, and I came up—both shows! It was Kentucky Straight Bourbon. A very generous fellow, he gave souvenirs. (*He pulls from his back pocket a shimmering rainbow-colored scarf.*) He gave me this. This is his magic scarf. You can have it, Laura. You wave it over a canary cage and you get a bowl of gold-fish. You wave it over the gold-fish bowl and they fly away canaries. . . . But the wonderfullest trick of all was the coffin trick. We nailed him into a coffin and he got out of the coffin without removing one nail. (*They enter.*) There is a trick that would come in handy for me—get me out of this 2 by 4 situation! (*Flops onto day-bed and starts removing shoes.*)

LAURA. Tom—shhh!

TOM. What're you shushing me for?

LAURA. You'll wake up Mother.

TOM. Goody goody! Pay 'er back for all those "Rise an' Shines." (*Lies down groaning.*) You know it don't take much intelligence to get yourself into a nailed-up coffin, Laura. But who in hell ever got himself out of one without removing one nail? (*As if in answer, the father's grinning photograph lights up. Laura exits up L. Lights fade except for blue glow in dining-room. Pause after lights fade, then clock chimes six times. This is followed by the alarm clock. Dim in fore-stage.*)

ACT I

SCENE 5

Scene is the same. Immediately following. The church-bell is heard striking six. At the sixth stroke the alarm-clock goes off in Amanda's room off R. of dining-room and after a few moments we hear her calling, "Rise and shine! Rise and shine! Laura, go tell your brother to rise and shine!"

TOM. (*Sitting up slowly in day-bed.*) I'll rise—but I won't shine. (*The light increases.*)

AMANDA. (*Offstage.*) Laura, tell your brother his coffee is ready. (*Laura, fully dressed, a cape over her shoulders, slips into living-room. Tom is still in bed, covered with blanket, having taken off only shoes and coat.*)

LAURA. Tom!—It's nearly seven. Don't make Mother nervous. (*He stares at her stupidly. Beseechingly.*) Tom, speak to Mother this morning. Make up with her, apologize, speak to her!

TOM. (*Putting on shoes.*) She won't to me. It's her that started not speaking.

LAURA. If you just say you're sorry she'll start speaking.

TOM. Her not speaking—is that such a tragedy?

LAURA. Please—please!

AMANDA. (*Calling offstage R. from kitchen.*) Laura, are you going to do what I asked you to do, or do I have to get dressed and go out myself?

LAURA. Going, going—soon as I get on my coat! (*She rises and crosses to door R.*) Butter and what else? (*To Amanda.*)

AMANDA. (*Offstage.*) Just butter. Tell them to charge it.

LAURA. Mother, they make such faces when I do that.

AMANDA. (*Offstage.*) Sticks and stones can break our bones, but the expression on Mr. Garfinkel's face won't harm us! Tell your brother his coffee is getting cold.

LAURA. (*At door R.*) Do what I asked you, will you, will you, Tom? (*He looks sullenly away.*)

AMANDA. Laura, go now or just don't go at all!

LAURA. (*Rushing out R.*) Going—going! (*A second later she cries out. Falls on fire-escape landing. Tom springs up and crosses to door R. Amanda rushes anxiously in from dining-room, puts dishes on dining-room table. Tom opens door R.*)

TOM. Laura?

LAURA. I'm all right. I slipped, but I'm all right. (*Goes up R. alley, out of sight.*)

AMANDA. (*On fire-escape.*) I tell you if anybody falls down and breaks a leg on those fire-escape steps, the landlord ought to be

27

sued for every cent he —— (*Sees Tom.*) Who are you? (*Leaves fire-escape landing, crosses to dining-room and returns with bowls, coffee cup, cream, etc. Puts them on small table* R. *of day-bed, crosses to armchair, sits. Counts* 3. *MUSIC CUE* #9. *As Tom re-enters* R., *listlessly for his coffee, she turns her back to him, as she sits in armchair. The light on her face with its aged but childish features is cruelly sharp, satirical as a Daumier print. Tom glances sheepishly but sullenly at her averted figure and sits on day-bed next to the food. The coffee is scalding hot, he sips it and gasps and spits it back in the cup. At his gasp, Amanda catches her breath and half turns. Then catches herself and turns away. Tom blows on his coffee, glancing sidewise at his mother. She clears her throat. Tom clears his. He starts to rise. Sinks back down again, scratches his head, clears his throat again. Amanda coughs. Tom raises his cup in both hands to blow on it, his eyes staring over the rim of it at his mother for several moments. Then he slowly sets the cup down and awkwardly and hesitantly rises from day-bed.*)

TOM. (*Hoarsely.*) I'm sorry, Mother. I'm sorry for all those things I said. I didn't mean it. I apologize.

AMANDA. (*Sobbingly.*) My devotion has made me a witch and so I make myself hateful to my children!

TOM. No, you don't.

AMANDA. I worry so much, I don't sleep, it makes me nervous!

TOM. (*Gently.*) I understand that.

AMANDA. You know I've had to put up a solitary battle all these years. But you're my right hand bower! Now don't fail me. Don't fall down.

TOM. (*Gently.*) I try, Mother.

AMANDA. (*With great enthusiasm.*) That's all right! You just keep on trying and you're bound to succeed. Why, you're—you're just full of natural endowments! Both my children are—they're very precious children and I've got an awful lot to be thankful for; you just must promise me one thing. (*MUSIC CUE* #9 STOPS.*)

TOM. What is it, Mother?

AMANDA. Promise me you're never going to become a drunkard!

TOM. I promise, Mother. I won't ever become a drunkard, Mother.

AMANDA. That's what frightened me so, that you'd be drinking! Eat a bowl of Purina.

TOM. Just coffee, Mother.

AMANDA. Shredded Wheat Biscuit?

TOM. No, no, Mother, just coffee.

AMANDA. You can't put in a day's work on an empty stomach. You've got ten minutes—don't gulp! Drinking too-hot liquids makes cancer of the stomach. . . . Put cream in.

TOM. No, thank you.

AMANDA. To cool it.

TOM. No! No, thank you, I want it black.

AMANDA. I know, but it's not good for you. We have to do all that we can to build ourselves up. In these trying times we live in, all that we have to cling to is—each other. . . . That's why it's so important to —— Tom, I—I sent out your sister so I could discuss something with you. If you hadn't spoken I would have spoken to you. (*Sits down.*)

TOM. (*Gently.*) What is it, Mother, that you want to discuss?

AMANDA. Laura! (*Tom puts his cup down slowly.* MUSIC CUE #10.)

TOM. —Oh.—Laura . . .

AMANDA. (*Touching his sleeve.*) You know how Laura is. So quiet but—still water runs deep! She notices things and I think she—broods about them. (*Tom looks up.*) A few days ago I came in and she was crying.

TOM. What about?

AMANDA. You.

TOM. Me?

AMANDA. She has an idea that you're not happy here. (MUSIC CUE #10 STOPS.)

TOM. What gave her that idea?

AMANDA. What gives her any idea? However, you do act strangely. (*Tom slaps cup down on small table.*) I—I'm not criticizing, understand that! I know your ambitions do not lie in the warehouse, that like everybody in the whole wide world—you've had to—make sacrifices, but—Tom—Tom—life's not easy, it calls for—Spartan endurance! There's so many things in my heart that I cannot describe to you! I've never told you but I—loved your father . . .

TOM. (*Gently.*) I know that, Mother.

AMANDA. And you—when I see you taking after his ways! Staying out late—and—well, you had been drinking the night you were in that—terrifying condition! Laura says that you hate the

29

apartment and that you go out nights to get away from it! Is that true, Tom?

TOM. No. You say there's so much in your heart that you can't describe to me. That's true of me, too. There's so much in my heart that I can't describe to you! So let's respect each other's ——

AMANDA. But, why—why, Tom—are you always so restless? Where do you go to, nights?

TOM. I—go to the movies.

AMANDA. Why do you go to the movies so much, Tom?

TOM. I go to the movies because—I like adventure. Adventure is something I don't have much of at work, so I go to the movies.

AMANDA. But, Tom, you go to the movies entirely too much!

TOM. I like a lot of adventure. (*Amanda looks baffled, then hurt. As the familiar inquisition resumes he becomes hard and impatient again. Amanda slips back into her querulous attitude toward him.*)

AMANDA. Most young men find adventure in their careers.

TOM. Then most young men are not employed in a warehouse.

AMANDA. The world is full of young men employed in warehouses and offices and factories.

TOM. Do all of them find adventure in their careers?

AMANDA. They do or they do without it! Not everybody has a craze for adventure.

TOM. Man is by instinct a lover, a hunter, a fighter, and none of those instincts are given much play at the warehouse!

AMANDA. Man is by instinct! Don't quote instinct to me! Instinct is something that people have got away from! It belongs to animals! Christian adults don't want it!

TOM. What do Christian adults want, then, Mother?

AMANDA. Superior things! Things of the mind and the spirit! Only animals have to satisfy instincts! Surely your aims are somewhat higher than theirs! Than monkeys—pigs ——

TOM. I reckon they're not.

AMANDA. You're joking. However, that isn't what I wanted to discuss.

TOM. (*Rising.*) I haven't much time.

AMANDA. (*Pushing his shoulders.*) Sit down.

TOM. You want me to punch in red at the warehouse, Mother?

AMANDA. You have five minutes. I want to talk about Laura.

TOM. All right! What about Laura?

AMANDA. We have to be making some plans and provisions for her. She's older than you, two years, and nothing has happened.

She just drifts along doing nothing. It frightens me terribly how she just drifts along.

TOM. I guess she's the type that people call home girls.

AMANDA. There's no such type, and if there is, it's a pity! That is unless the home is hers, with a husband!

TOM. What?

AMANDA. (*Crossing* D. R. *to armchair.*) Oh, I can see the hand-writing on the wall as plain as I see the nose in front of my face! It's terrifying! More and more you remind me of your father! He was out all (*Sits in armchair.*) hours without explanation!—Then left! Good-bye! And me with the bag to hold. I saw that letter you got from the Merchant Marine. I know what you're dreaming of. I'm not standing here blindfolded. Very well, then. Then do it! But not till there's somebody to take your place.

TOM. What do you mean?

AMANDA. I mean that as soon as Laura has got somebody to take care of her, married, a home of her own, independent—why, then you'll be free to go wherever you please, (*Rises, crosses to Tom.*) on land, on sea, whichever way the wind blows you! But until that time you've got to look out for your sister. (*Crosses* R. *behind armchair.*) I don't say me because I'm old and don't matter! I say for your sister because she's young and dependent. I put her in business college—a dismal failure! Frightened her so it made her sick at the stomach. I took her over to the Young People's League at the church. Another fiasco. She spoke to nobody, nobody spoke to her. (*Sits armchair.*) Now all she does is fool with those pieces of glass and play those worn-out records. What kind of a life is that for a girl to lead?

TOM. What can I do about it?

AMANDA. Overcome selfishness! Self, self, self is all that you ever think of! (*Tom springs up and crosses* R. *to get his coat and put it on. It is ugly and bulky. He pulls on a cap with earmuffs.*) Where is your muffler? Put your wool muffler on! (*He snatches it angrily from the hook and tosses it around his neck and pulls both ends tight.*) Tom! I haven't said what I had in mind to ask you.

TOM. I'm too late to ——

AMANDA. (*Catching his arm—very importunately. Then shyly.*) Down at the warehouse, aren't there some—nice young men?

TOM. No!

AMANDA. There must be—some . . .

TOM. Mother —— (*Gesture.*)

AMANDA. Find out one that's clean-living—doesn't drink and—ask him out for sister!

TOM. What?

AMANDA. For sister! To meet! Get acquainted!

TOM. (*Stamping to door* R.) Oh, my go-osh!

AMANDA. Will you? (*He opens door. Imploringly.*) Will you? (*He starts out.*) Will you? Will you, dear? (*Tom exits up alley* R. *Amanda is on fire-escape landing.*)

TOM. (*Calling back.*) Yes!

AMANDA. (*Re-entering* R. *and crossing to phone.* MUSIC CUE #11.) Ella Cartwright? Ella, this is Amanda Wingfield. First, first, how's that kidney trouble? Oh, it has? It has come back? Well, you're just a Christian martyr, you're just a Christian martyr. I was noticing in my little red book that your subscription to the "Companion" has run out just when that wonderful new serial by Bessie Mae Harper was starting. It's all about the horsey set on Long Island. Oh, you have? You have read it? Well, how do you think it turns out? Oh, no. Bessie Mae Harper never lets you down. Oh, of course, we have to have complications. You have to have complications—oh, you can't have a story without them—but Bessie Mae Harper always leaves you with such an uplift —— What's the matter, Ella? You sound so mad. Oh, because it's seven o'clock in the morning. Oh, Ella, I forgot that you never got up until nine. I forgot that anybody in the world was allowed to sleep as late as that. I can't say any more than I'm sorry, can I? Oh, you will? You're going to take that subscription from me anyhow? Well, bless you, Ella, bless you, bless you, bless you. (MUSIC #11 *fades into* MUSIC CUE #11-A, *dance music, and continues into next scene. Dim out lights.* MUSIC CUE #11-A.)

ACT I

SCENE 6

SCENE: *The same.—Only* R. *alley lighted, with dim light.*

TOM. (*Enters down* R. *and stands as before, leaning against grill-work, with cigarette, wearing merchant sailor coat and cap.*) Across the alley was the Paradise Dance Hall. Evenings in spring they'd open all the doors and windows and the music would come outside. Sometimes they'd turn out all the lights except for a large glass sphere that hung from the ceiling. It would turn slowly about and filter the dusk with delicate rainbow colors. Then the orchestra would play a waltz or a tango, something that had a slow and sensuous rhythm. The young couples would come outside, to the relative privacy of the alley. You could see them kissing behind ashpits and telephone poles. This was the compensation for lives that passed like mine, without change or adventure. Changes and adventure, however, were imminent this year. They were waiting around the corner for all these dancing kids. Suspended in the mist over Berchtesgaden, caught in the folds of Chamberlain's umbrella —— In Spain there was Guernica! Here there was only hot swing music and liquor, dance halls, bars, and movies, and sex that hung in the gloom like a chandelier and flooded the world with brief, deceptive rainbows. . . . While these unsuspecting kids danced to "Dear One, The World is Waiting for the Sunrise." All the world was really waiting for bombardments. (MUSIC #11-A stops. Dim in dining-room: faint glow. Amanda is seen in dining-room.)

AMANDA. Tom, where are you?

TOM. (Standing as before.) I came out to smoke. (Exit R. into the wings, where he again changes coats and leaves hat.)

AMANDA. (Tom re-enters and stands on fire-escape landing, smoking. He opens door for Amanda, who sits on bassock on landing.) Oh, you smoke too much. A pack a day at fifteen cents a pack. How much would that be in a month? Thirty times fifteen? It wouldn't be very much. Well, it would be enough to help towards a night-school course in accounting at the Washington U! Wouldn't that be lovely?

TOM. I'd rather smoke.

AMANDA. I know! That's the tragedy of you. This fire-escape landing is a poor excuse for the porch we used to have. What are you looking at?

TOM. The moon.

AMANDA. Is there a moon this evening?

TOM. It's rising over Garfinkel's Delicatessen.

AMANDA. Oh! So it is! Such a little silver slipper of a moon. Have you made a wish on it?

TOM. Um-mm.

AMANDA. What did you wish?

TOM. That's a secret.

AMANDA. All right, I won't tell you what I wished, either. I can keep a secret, too. I can be just as mysterious as you.

TOM. I bet I can guess what you wished.

AMANDA. Why, is my head transparent?

TOM. You're not a sphinx.

AMANDA. No, I don't have secrets. I'll tell you what I wished for on the moon. Success and happiness for my precious children. I wish for that whenever there's a moon, and when there isn't a moon, I wish for it, too.

TOM. I thought perhaps you wished for a gentleman caller.

AMANDA. Why do you say that?

TOM. Don't you remember asking me to fetch one?

AMANDA. I remember suggesting that it would be nice for your sister if you brought home some nice young man from the warehouse. I think that I've made that suggestion more than once.

TOM. Yes, you have made it repeatedly.

AMANDA. Well?

TOM. We are going to have one.

AMANDA. *What?*

TOM. A gentleman caller!

AMANDA. You mean you have asked some nice young man to come over? (*Rising from stool, facing Tom.*)

TOM. I've asked him to dinner.

AMANDA. You really did?

TOM. I did.

AMANDA. And did he—accept?

TOM. He did!

AMANDA. He did?

TOM. He did.

AMANDA. Well, isn't that lovely!

TOM. I thought that you would be pleased.

AMANDA. It's definite, then?

TOM. Oh, very definite.

AMANDA. How soon?

TOM. Pretty soon.

AMANDA. How soon?

TOM. Quite soon.

AMANDA. How soon?

TOM. Very, very soon.

AMANDA. Every time I want to know anything you start going on like that.

TOM. What do you want to know?

AMANDA. Go ahead and guess. Go ahead and guess.

TOM. All right, I'll guess. You want to know when the gentleman caller's coming—he's coming tomorrow.

AMANDA. Tomorrow? Oh, no, I can't do anything about tomorrow. I can't do anything about tomorrow.

TOM. Why not?

AMANDA. That doesn't give me any time.

TOM. Time for what?

AMANDA. Time for preparations. Oh, you should have phoned me the minute you asked him—the minute he accepted!

TOM. You don't have to make any fuss.

AMANDA. Of course I have to make a fuss! I can't have a man coming into a place that's all sloppy. It's got to be thrown together properly. I certainly have to do some fast thinking by tomorrow night, too.

TOM. I don't see why you have to think at all.

AMANDA. That's because you just don't know. (*Enter living-room, crosses to C. Dim in living-room.*) You just don't know, that's all. We can't have a gentleman caller coming into a pig-sty! Now, let's see. Oh, I've got those three pieces of wedding silver left. I'll polish that up. I wonder how that old lace tablecloth is holding up all these years? We can't wear anything. We haven't got it. We haven't got anything to wear. We haven't got it. (*Goes back to door R.*)

TOM. Mother! This boy is no one to make a fuss over.

AMANDA. (*Crossing to C.*) I don't know how you can say that when this is the first gentleman caller your little sister's ever had! I think it's pathetic that that little girl has never had a single gentleman caller! Come on inside! Come on inside!

TOM. What for?

AMANDA. I want to ask you a few things.

TOM. (*From doorway R.*) If you're going to make a fuss, I'll call the whole thing off. I'll call the boy up and tell him not to come.

AMANDA. No! You mustn't ever do that. People hate broken engagements. They have no place to go. Come on inside. Come on inside. Will you come inside when I ask you to come inside? Sit down. (*Tom comes into living-room.*)

TOM. Any particular place you want me to sit?

AMANDA. Oh! Sit anywhere. (*Tom sits armchair* R.) Look! What am I going to do about that? (*Looking at day-bed.*) Did you ever see anything look so sad? I know, I'll get a bright piece of cretonne. That won't cost much. And I made payments on a floor lamp. So I'll have that sent out! And I can put a bright cover on the chair. I wish I had time to paper the walls. What's his name?

TOM. His name is O'Connor.

AMANDA. O'Connor—he's Irish and tomorrow's Friday—that means fish. Well, that's all right, I'll make a salmon loaf and some mayonnaise dressing for it. Where did you meet him? (*Crosses to day-bed and sits.*)

TOM. At the warehouse, of course. Where else would I meet him?

AMANDA. Well, I don't know. Does he drink?

TOM. What made you ask me that?

AMANDA. Because your father did.

TOM. Now, don't get started on that!

AMANDA. He drinks, then.

TOM. No, not that I know of.

AMANDA. You have to find out. There's nothing I want less for my daughter than a man who drinks.

TOM. Aren't you being a little bit premature? After all, poor Mr. O'Connor hasn't even appeared on the scene yet.

AMANDA. But he will tomorrow. To meet your sister. And what do I know about his character? (*Rises and crosses to Tom who is still in armchair, smooths his hair.*)

TOM. (*Submitting grimly.*) Now what are you up to?

AMANDA. I always did hate that cowlick. I never could understand why it won't sit down by itself.

TOM. Mother, I want to tell you something and I mean it sincerely right straight from my heart. There's a lot of boys who meet girls which they don't marry!

AMANDA. You know you always had me worried because you could never stick to a subject. (*Crosses to day-bed.*) What I want to know is what's his position at the warehouse?

TOM. He's a shipping clerk.

AMANDA. Oh! Shipping clerk! Well, that's fairly important.

That's where you'd be if you had more get-up. How much does he earn? (*Sits on day-bed.*)

TOM. I have no way of knowing that for sure. I judge his salary to be approximately eighty-five dollars a month.

AMANDA. Eighty-five dollars? Well, that's not princely.

TOM. It's twenty dollars more than I make.

AMANDA. I know that. Oh, how well I know that! How well I know that! Eighty-five dollars a month. No. It can't be done. A family man can never get by on eighty-five dollars a month.

TOM. Mother, Mr. O'Connor is not a family man.

AMANDA. Well, he might be some time in the future, mightn't he?

TOM. Oh, I see. . . . Plans and provisions.

AMANDA. You are the only young man that I know of who ignores the fact that the future becomes the present, the present the past, and the past turns into everlasting regret if you don't plan for it.

TOM. I will think that over and see what I can make of it!

AMANDA. Don't be supercilious with your mother! Tell me some more about this.—What do you call him? Mr. O'Connor, Mr O'Connor. He must have another name besides Mr.——?

TOM. His full name is James D. O'Connor. The D. is for Delaney.

AMANDA. Delaney? Irish on both sides and he doesn't drink?

TOM. (*Rises from armchair.*) Shall I call him up and ask him? (*Starts toward phone.*)

AMANDA. (*Crossing to phone.*) No!

TOM. I'll call him up and tell him you want to know if he drinks. (*Picks up phone.*)

AMANDA. (*Taking phone away from him.*) No, you can't do that. You have to be discreet about that subject. When I was a girl in Blue Mountain if it was (*Tom sits on R. of day-bed.*) suspected that a young man was drinking and any girl was receiving his attentions—if any girl *was* receiving his attentions, she'd go to the minister of his church and ask about his character—or her father, if her father was living, then it was his duty to go to the minister of his church and ask about his character, and that's how young girls in Blue Mountain were kept from making tragic mistakes. (*Picture dims in and out.*) [6]

[6] See note p. 19.

TOM. How come you made such a tragic one?

AMANDA. Oh, I don't know how he did it, but that face fooled everybody. All he had to do was grin and the world was bewitched. (*Behind day-bed, crosses to armchair.*) I don't know of anything more tragic than a young girl just putting herself at the mercy of a handsome appearance, and I hope Mr. O'Connor is *not* too good-looking.

TOM. As a matter of fact he isn't. His face is covered with freckles and he has a very large nose.

AMANDA. He's not right-down homely?

TOM. No. I wouldn't say right-down—homely—medium homely, I'd say.

AMANDA. Well, if a girl had any sense she'd look for character in a man anyhow.

TOM. That's what I've always said, Mother.

AMANDA. You've always said it—you've always said it! How could you've always said it when you never even thought about it?

TOM. Aw, don't be so suspicious of me.

AMANDA. I am. I'm suspicious of every word that comes out of your mouth, when you talk to me, but I want to know about this young man. Is he up and coming?

TOM. Yes. I really do think he goes in for self-improvement.

AMANDA. What makes you think it?

TOM. He goes to night school.

AMANDA. Well, what does he do there at night school?

TOM. He's studying radio engineering and public speaking.

AMANDA. Oh! Public speaking! Oh, that shows, that shows that he intends to be an executive some day—and radio engineering. Well, that's coming . . . huh?

TOM. I think it's here.

AMANDA. Well, those are all very illuminating facts. (*Crosses to back of armchair.*) Facts that every mother should know about any young man calling on her daughter, seriously or not.

TOM. Just one little warning, Mother. I didn't tell him anything about Laura. I didn't let on we had dark ulterior motives. I just said, "How about coming home to dinner some time?" and he said, "Fine," and that was the whole conversation.

AMANDA. I bet it was, too. I tell you, sometimes you can be as eloquent as an oyster. However, when he sees how pretty and sweet that child is, he's going to be, well, he's going to be very glad he was asked over here to have some dinner. (*Sits in armchair.*)

TOM. Mother, just one thing. You won't expect too much of Laura, will you?

AMANDA. I don't know what you mean. (*Tom crosses slowly to Amanda. He stands for a moment, looking at her. Then—*)

TOM. Well, Laura seems all those things to you and me because she's ours and we love her. We don't even notice she's crippled any more.

AMANDA. Don't use that word.

TOM. Mother, you have to face the facts; she is, and that's not all.

AMANDA. What do you mean "that's not all"? (*Tom kneels by her chair.*)

TOM. Mother—you know that Laura is very different from other girls.

AMANDA. Yes, I do know that, and I think that difference is all in her favor, too.

TOM. Not quite all—in the eyes of others—strangers—she's terribly shy. She lives in a world of her own and those things make her seem a little peculiar to people outside the house.

AMANDA. Don't use that word peculiar.

TOM. You have to face the facts.—She is.

AMANDA. I don't know in what way she's peculiar. (MUSIC CUE #12, till curtain. *Tom pauses a moment for music, then—*)

TOM. Mother, Laura lives in a world of little glass animals. She plays old phonograph records—and—that's about all —— (*Tom rises slowly, goes quietly out the door R., leaving it open, and exits slowly up the alley. Amanda rises, goes on to fire-escape landing R., looks at moon.*)

AMANDA. Laura! Laura! (*Laura answers from kitchen R.*)

LAURA. Yes, Mother.

AMANDA. Let those dishes go and come in front! (*Laura appears with dish towel. Gaily.*) Laura, come here and make a wish on the moon!

LAURA. (*Entering from kitchen R. and comes down to fire-escape landing.*) Moon—moon?

AMANDA. A little silver slipper of a moon. Look over your left shoulder, Laura, and make a wish! (*Laura looks faintly puzzled*

as if called out of sleep. Amanda seizes her shoulders and turns her at an angle on the fire-escape landing.) Now! Now, darling, wish!
LAURA. What shall I wish for, Mother?
AMANDA. *(Her voice trembling and her eyes suddenly filling with tears.)* Happiness! And just a little bit of good fortune! *(The stage dims out.)*

CURTAIN

ACT II

SCENE 7

SCENE: *The same.*
Inner curtains closed between dining-room and living-room. Interiors of both rooms are dark as at beginning of play. Tom has on the same jacket and cap as at first. Same dance-hall music as CUE #1, *fading as Tom begins.*

TOM. (*Discovered leaning against grill on fire-escape landing, as before, and smoking.*) And so the following evening I brought Jim home to dinner. I had known Jim slightly in high school. In high school, Jim was a hero. He had tremendous Irish good nature and vitality with the scrubbed and polished look of white chinaware. He seemed to move in a continual spotlight. He was a star in basketball, captain of the debating club, president of the senior class and the glee club, and he sang the male lead in the annual light opera. He was forever running or bounding, never just walking. He seemed always just at the point of defeating the law of gravity. He was shooting with such velocity through his adolescence that you would just logically expect him to arrive at nothing short of the White House by the time he was thirty. But Jim apparently ran into more interference after his graduation from high school because his speed had definitely slowed. And so, at this particular time in our lives he was holding a job that wasn't much better than mine. He was the only one at the warehouse with whom I was on friendly terms. I was valuable to Jim as someone who could remember his former glory, who had seen him win basketball games and the silver cup in debating. He knew of my secret practice of retiring to a cabinet of the washroom to work on poems whenever business was slack in the warehouse. He called me Shakespeare. And while the other boys in the warehouse regarded me with suspicious hostility, Jim took a humorous attitude toward me. Gradually his attitude began to affect the other boys and their hostility wore off. And so, after a time they began to smile at me too, as

41

people smile at some oddly fashioned dog that trots across their path at some distance. I knew that Jim and Laura had known each other in high school because I had heard my sister Laura speak admiringly of Jim's voice. I didn't know if Jim would remember her or not. Because in high school Laura had been as unobtrusive as Jim had been astonishing. And, if he did remember Laura, it was not as my sister, for when I asked him home to dinner, he smiled and said, "You know, a funny thing, Shakespeare, I never thought of you as having folks!" Well, he was about to discover that I did. . . . (MUSIC CUE #13. *Tom exits* R. *Interior living-room lights dim in. Amanda is sitting on small table* R. *of day-bed sewing on hem on Laura's dress. Laura stands facing the door* R. *Amanda has worked like a Turk in preparation for the gentleman caller. The results are astonishing. The new floor lamp with its rose-silk shade is in place,* R. *of living-room next to wall, a colored paper lantern conceals the broken light fixture in the ceiling, chintz covers are on chairs and sofa, a pair of new sofa pillows make their initial appearance. Laura stands in the middle of room with lifted arms while Amanda crouches before her, adjusting the hem of the new dress, devout and ritualistic. The dress is colored and designed by memory. The arrangement of Laura's hair is changed, it is softer and more becoming. A fragile, unearthly prettiness has come out in Laura, she is like a piece of translucent glass touched by light, given a momentary radiance, not actual, not lasting. Amanda, still seated, is sewing Laura's dress. Laura is standing* R. *of Amanda.*)

AMANDA. Why are you trembling so, Laura?

LAURA. Mother, you've made me so nervous!

AMANDA. Why, how have I made you nervous?

LAURA. By all this fuss! You make it seem so important.

AMANDA. I don't understand you at all, honey. Every time I try to do anything for you that's the least bit different you just seem to set yourself against it. Now take a look at yourself. (*Laura starts for door* R.) No, wait! Wait just a minute—I forgot something. (*Picks two powder puffs from day-bed.*)

LAURA. What is it?

AMANDA. A couple of improvements. (*Business with powder puffs.*) When I was a girl we had round little lacy things like that and we called them "Gay Deceivers."

LAURA. I won't wear them!

42

AMANDA. Of course you'll wear them.

LAURA. Why should I?

AMANDA. Well, to tell you the truth, honey, you're just a little bit flat-chested.

LAURA. You make it seem like we were setting a trap.

AMANDA. We are. All pretty girls are a trap and men expect them to be traps. Now look at yourself in that galss. (*Laura crosses* R. *Looks at mirror, invisible to audience, which is in darkness up* R. *of* R. *door.*) See? You look just like an angel on a postcard. Isn't that lovely? Now you just wait. I'm going to dress myself up. You're going to be astonished at your mother's appearance. (END OF MUSIC CUE. *End of Music Cue leads into dance music,*[1] *which then leads in* MUSIC CUE #14, *a few lines below, at stage direction. Amanda exits through curtains up-stage off* L. *in dining-room. Laura looks in mirror for a moment. Removes "Gay Deceivers," hides them under mattress of day-bed. Sits on small table* R. *of day-bed for a moment, goes out to fire-escape landing, listens to dance music, until Amanda's entrance. Amanda, off.*) I found an old dress in the trunk. But what do you know? I had to do a lot to it but it broke my heart when I had to let it out. Now, Laura, just look at your mother. Oh, no! Laura, come look at me now! (*Enters dining-room* L. *door. Comes down through living-room curtain to living-room* C. MUSIC CUE #14.)

LAURA. (*Re-enters from fire-escape landing. Sits on* L. *arm of armchair.*) Oh, Mother, how lovely! (*Amanda wears a girlish frock. She carries a bunch of jonquils.*)

AMANDA. (*Standing* C., *holding flowers.*) It used to be. It used to be. It had a lot of flowers on it, but they got awful tired so I had to take them all off. I led the cotillion in this dress years ago. I won the cake-walk twice at Sunset Hill, and I wore it to the Governor's ball in Jackson. You should have seen your mother. You should have seen your mother how she just sashayed around (*Crossing around* L. *of day-bed back to* C.) the ballroom, just like that. I had it on the day I met your father. I had malaria fever, too. The change of climate from East Tennessee to the Delta—weakened my resistance. Not enough to be dangerous, just enough to make me restless and giddy. Oh, it was lovely. Invitations poured in from all over. My mother said, "You can't go any place because you have a fever. You have to stay in bed." I said I wouldn't and I

---

[1] Optional. Not on regular records of incidental music to the play.

took quinine and kept on going and going. Dances every evening and long rides in the country in the afternoon and picnics. That country—that country—so lovely—so lovely in May, all lacy with dogwood and simply flooded with jonquils. My mother said, "You can't bring any more jonquils in this house." I said, "I will," and I kept on bringing them in anyhow. Whenever I saw them I said, "Wait a minute, I see jonquils," and I'd make my gentlemen callers get out of the carriage and help me gather some. To tell you the truth, Laura, it got to be a kind of a joke. "Look out," they'd say, "here comes that girl and we'll have to spend the afternoon picking jonquils." My mother said, "You can't bring any more jonquils in the house, there aren't any more vases to hold them." "That's quite all right," I siad, "I can hold some myself." Malaria fever, your father and jonquils. (*Amanda puts jonquils in Laura's lap and goes out on to fire-escape landing. MUSIC CUE #14 STOPS. THUN-DER HEARD.*) I hope they get here before it starts to rain. I gave your brother a little extra change so he and Mr. O'Connor could take the service car home. (*Laura puts flowers on armchair R., and crosses to door R.*)

LAURA. Mother!

AMANDA. What's the matter now? (*Re-entering room.*)

LAURA. What did you say his name was?

AMANDA. O'Connor. Why?

LAURA. What is his first name?

AMANDA. (*Crosses to armchair R.*) I don't remember —— Oh, yes, I do too—it was—Jim! (*Picks up flowers.*)

LAURA. Oh, Mother, not Jim O'Connor!

AMANDA. Yes, that was it, it was Jim! I've never known a Jim that wasn't nice. (*Crosses L., behind day-bed, puts flowers ni vase.*)

LAURA. Are you sure his name was Jim O'Connor?

AMANDA. Why, sure I'm sure. Why?

LAURA. Is he the one that Tom used to know in high school?

AMANDA. He didn't say so. I think he just got to know him— (*Sits on day-bed.*) at the warehouse.

LAURA. There was a Jim O'Connor we both knew in high school. If that is the one that Tom is bringing home to dinner —— Oh, Mother, you'd have to excuse me, I wouldn't come to the table!

AMANDA. What's this now? What sort of silly talk is this?

LAURA. You asked me once if I'd ever liked a boy. Don't you remember I showed you this boy's picture?

44

AMANDA. You mean the boy in the year-book?

LAURA. Yes, that boy.

AMANDA. Laura, Laura, were you in love with that boy?

LAURA. (Crosses to R. of armchair.) I don't know, Mother. All I know is that I couldn't sit at the table if it was him.

AMANDA. (Rises, crosses L. and works up L. of day-bed.) It won't be him! It isn't the least bit likely. But whether it is or not, you will come to the table—you will not be excused.

LAURA. I'll have to be, Mother.

AMANDA. (Behind day-bed.) I don't intend to humor your silliness, Laura. I've had too much from you and your brother, both. So just sit down and compose yourself till they come. Tom has forgotten his key, so you'll have to let them in when they arrive.

LAURA. Oh, Mother—you answer the door! (Sits chair R.)

AMANDA. How can I when I haven't even finished making the mayonnaise dressing for the salmon?

LAURA. Oh, Mother, please answer the door, don't make me do it! (Thunder heard off-stage.)

AMANDA. Honey, do be reasonable! What's all this fuss about —just one gentleman caller—that's all—just one! (Exits through living-room curtains. Tom and Jim enter alley R., climb fire-escape steps to landing and wait outside of closed door. Hearing them approach, Laura rises with a panicky gesture. She retreats to living-room curtains. The doorbell rings. Laura catches her breath and touches her throat. More thunder heard off-stage.)

AMANDA. (Off-stage.) Laura, sweetheart, the door!

LAURA. Mother, please, you go to the door! (Starts for door R., then back.)

AMANDA. (Off-stage, in a fierce whisper.) What is the matter with you, you silly thing? (Enters through living-room curtains, and stands by day-bed.)

LAURA. Please you answer it, please.

AMANDA. Why have you chosen this moment to lose your mind? You go to that door.

LAURA. I can't.

AMANDA. Why can't you?

LAURA. Because I'm sick. (Crosses to L. end of day-bed and sits.)

AMANDA. You're sick! Am I sick? You and your brother have me puzzled to death. You can never act like normal children. Will you give me one good reason why you should be afraid to open a door? You go to that door. Laura Wingfield, you march straight to that door!

LAURA. (*Crosses to door* R.) Yes, Mother.

AMANDA. (*Stopping Laura.*) I've got to put courage in you, honey, for living. (*Exits through living-room curtains, and exits* R. *into kitchen. Laura opens door. Tom and Jim enter. Laura remains hidden in hall behind door.*)

TOM. Laura—(*Laura crosses* C.) this is Jim. Jim, this is my sister Laura.

JIM. I didn't know that Shakespeare had a sister! How are you, Laura?

LAURA. (*Retreating stiff and trembling. Shakes hands.*) How—how do you do?

JIM. Well, I'm okay! Your hand's *cold*, Laura! (*Tom puts hats on phone table.*)

LAURA. Yes, well—I've been playing the victrola. . . .

JIM. Must have been playing classical music on it. You ought to play a little hot swing music to warm you up. (*Laura crosses to phonograph. Tom crosses up to Laura. Laura starts phonograph* [2] —*looks at Jim. Exits through living-room curtains and goes off* L.)

JIM. What's the matter?

TOM. Oh—Laura? Laura is—is terribly shy. (*Crosses and sits day-bed.*)

JIM. (*Crosses down* C.) Shy, huh? Do you know it's unusual to meet a shy girl nowadays? I don't believe you ever mentioned you had a sister?

TOM. Well, now you know I have one. You want a piece of the paper?

JIM. (*Crosses to Tom.*) Uh-huh.

TOM. Comics?

JIM. Comics? Sports! (*Takes paper. Crosses, sits chair* R.) I see that Dizzy Dean is on his bad behavior.

TOM. (*Starts to door* R. *Goes out.*) Really?

JIM. Yeah. Where are you going? (*As Tom reaches steps* R. *of fire-escape landing.*)

TOM. (*Calling from fire-escape landing.*) Out on the terrace to smoke.

JIM. (*Rises, leaving newspaper in armchair, goes over to turn off*

[2] A worn record of *Dardanella* or some other popular tune of the 1920's.

46

victrola. Crosses R. *Exits to fire-escape landing.*) You know, Shakespeare—I'm going to sell you a bill of goods!

TOM. What goods?

JIM. A course I'm taking.

TOM. What course?

JIM. A course in public speaking! You know you and me, we're not the warehouse type.

TOM. Thanks—that's good news. What has public speaking got to do with it?

JIM. It fits you for—executive positions!

TOM. Oh.

JIM. I tell you it's done a helluva lot for me.

TOM. In what respect?

JIM. In all respects. Ask yourself: what's the difference between you and me and the guys in the office down front? Brains?—No! —Ability?—No! Then what? Primarily, it amounts to just one single thing ——

TOM. What is that one thing?

JIM. Social poise! The ability to square up to somebody and hold your own on any social level!

AMANDA. (*Off-stage.*) Tom?

TOM. Yes, Mother?

AMANDA. Is that you and Mr. O'Connor?

TOM. Yes, Mother.

AMANDA. Make yourselves comfortable.

TOM. We will.

AMANDA. Ask Mr. O'Connor if he would like to wash his hands?

JIM. No, thanks, ma'am—I took care of that down at the warehouse. Tom?

TOM. Huh?

JIM. Mr. Mendoza was speaking to me about you.

TOM. Favorably?

JIM. What do you think?

TOM. Well ——

JIM. You're going to be out of a job if you don't wake up.

TOM. I'm waking up ——

JIM. Yeah, but you show no signs.

TOM. The signs are interior. I'm just about to make a change. I'm right at the point of committing myself to a future that doesn't in-

47

clude the warehouse or Mr. Mendoza, or even a night school course in public speaking.

JIM. Now what are you gassing about?

TOM. I'm tired of the movies.

JIM. The movies!

TOM. Yes, movies! Look at them. (*He waves his hands.*) All of those glamorous people—having adventures—hogging it all, gobbling the whole thing up! You know what happens? People go to the *movies* instead of *moving*. Hollywood characters are supposed to have all the adventures for everybody in America, while everybody in America sits in a dark room and watches them having it! Yes, until there's a war. That's when adventure becomes available to the masses! Everyone's dish, not only Gable's! Then the people in the dark room come out of the dark room to have some adventures themselves—goody—goody! It's our turn now to go to the South Sea Island—to make a safari—to be exotic, far off . . . ! But I'm not patient. I don't want to wait till then. I'm tired of the movies and I'm about to move!

JIM. (*Incredulously.*) Move?

TOM. Yes.

JIM. When?

TOM. Soon!

JIM. Where? Where?

TOM. I'm starting to boil inside. I know I seem dreamy, but inside—well, I'm boiling! Whenever I pick up a shoe I shudder a little, thinking how short life is and what I am doing!—Whatever that means, I know it doesn't mean shoes—except as something to wear on a traveler's feet! (*Gets card from inside coat pocket.*) Look!

JIM. What?

TOM. I'm a member.

JIM. (*Reading.*) The Union of Merchant Seamen.

TOM. I paid my dues this month, instead of the electric light bill.

JIM. You'll regret it when they turn off the lights.

TOM. I won't be here.

JIM. Yeah, but how about your mother?

TOM. I'm like my father. The bastard son of a bastard. See how he grins? And he's been absent going on sixteen years.

JIM. You're just talking, you drip. How does your mother feel about it?

48

TOM. Sh! Here comes Mother! Mother's not acquainted with my plans!

AMANDA. (*Off-stage.*) Tom!

TOM. Yes, Mother?

AMANDA. (*Off-stage.*) Where are you all?

TOM. On the terrace, Mother.

AMANDA. (*Enters through living-room curtain and stands* c.) *Why don't you come in?* (*They start inside. She advances to them. Tom is distinctly shocked at her appearance. Even Jim blinks a little. He is making his first contact with girlish Southern vivacity and in spite of the night-school course in public speaking is somewhat thrown off the beam by the unexpected outlay of social charm. Certain responses are attempted by Jim but are swept aside by Amanda's gay laughter and chatter. Tom is embarrassed but after the first shock Jim reacts very warmly. Grins and chuckles, is altogether won over. Tom and Jim come in, leaving door open.*)

TOM. Mother, you look so pretty.

AMANDA. You know, that's the first compliment you ever paid me. I wish you'd look pleasant when you're about to say something pleasant, so I could expect it. Mr. O'Connor? (*Jim crosses to Amanda.*)

JIM. How do you do?

AMANDA. Well, well, well, so this is Mr. O'Connor? Introduction's entirely unnecessary. I've heard so much about you from my boy. I finally said to him, "Tom, good gracious, why don't you bring this paragon to supper finally? I'd like to meet this nice young man at the warehouse! Instead of just hearing you sing his praises so much?" I don't know why my son is so stand-offish—that's not Southern behavior. Let's sit down. (*Tom closes door, crosses* u. R., *stands. Jim and Amanda sit on day-bed, Jim,* R., *Amanda* L.) Let's sit down, and I think we could stand a little more air in here. Tom, leave the door open. I felt a nice fresh breeze a moment ago. Where has it gone to? Mmmm, so warm already! And not quite summer, even. We're going to burn up when summer really gets started. However, we're having—we're having a very light supper. I think light things are better fo'—for this time of year. The same as light clothes are. Light clothes and light food are what warm weather calls fo'. You know our blood gets so thick during th' winter—it takes a while fo' us to adjust ou'-

49

selves—when the season changes. . . . It's come so quick this year. I wasn't prepared. All of a sudden—Heavens! Already summer!—I ran to the trunk an'—pulled out this light dress—terribly old! Historical almost! But feels so good—so good and cool, why, y' know ——

TOM. Mother, how about our supper?

AMANDA. (*Rises, crosses* R. *to Tom.*) Honey, you go ask sister if supper is ready! You know that sister is in full charge of supper. Tell her you hungry boys are waiting for it. (*Tom exits through curtains and off* L. *Amanda turns to Jim.*) Have you met Laura?

JIM. Well, she came to the door.

AMANDA. She let you in?

JIM. Yes, ma'am.

AMANDA. (*Crossing to armchair and sitting.*) She's very pretty.

JIM. Oh, yes, ma'am.

AMANDA. It's rare for a girl as sweet an' pretty as Laura to be domestic! But Laura is, thank heavens, not only pretty but also very domestic. I'm not at all. I never was a bit. I never could make a thing but angel-food cake. Well, in the South we had so many servants. Gone, gone, gone. All vestige of gracious living! Gone completely! I wasn't prepared for what the future brought me. All of my gentlemen callers were sons of planters and so of course I assumed that I would be married to one and raise my family on a large piece of land with plenty of servants. But man proposes—and woman accepts the proposal!—To vary that old, old saying a little bit—I married no planter! I married a man who worked for the telephone company!—That gallantly smiling gentleman over there! (*Points to picture.*) A telephone man who—fell in love with long-distance!—Now he travels and I don't even know where!—But what am I going on for about my—tribulations? Tell me yours —I hope you don't have any! Tom?

TOM. (*Re-enters through living-room curtains from off* L.) Yes, Mother.

AMANDA. What about that supper?

TOM. Why, supper is on the table. (*Inner curtains between living-room and dining-room open. Lights dim up in dining-room, dim out in living-room.*)

AMANDA. Oh, so it is. (*Rises, crosses up to table* C. *in dining-room and chair* C.) How lovely. Where is Laura?

TOM. (*Going to chair* L. *and standing.*) Laura is not feeling too well and thinks maybe she'd better not come to the table.

AMANDA. Laura!

LAURA. (*Off-stage. Faintly.*) Yes, Mother? (*Tom gestures re: Jim.*)

AMANDA. Mr. O'Connor. (*Jim crosses up* L. *to table and to chair* L. *and stands.*)

JIM. Thank you, ma'am.

AMANDA. Laura, we can't say grace till you come to the table.

LAURA. (*Enters* U. L., *obviously quite faint, lips trembling, eyes wide and staring. Moves unsteadily toward dining-room table.*) Oh, Mother, I'm so sorry. (*Tom catches her as she feels faint. He takes her to day-bed in living-room.*)

AMANDA. (*As Laura lies down.*) Why, Laura, you are sick, darling! Laura—rest on the sofa. Well! (*To Jim.*) Standing over the hot stove made her ill!—I told her that it was just too warm this evening, but —— (*To Tom.*) Is Laura all right now?

TOM. She's better, Mother. (*Sits chair* L. *in dining-room. Thunder off-stage.*)

AMANDA. (*Returning to dining-room and sitting at table, as Jim does.*) My goodness, I suppose we're going to have a little rain! Tom, you say grace.

TOM. What?

AMANDA. What do we generally do before we have something to eat? We say grace, don't we?

TOM. For these and all Thy mercies—God's Holy Name be praised. (*Lights dim out.* MUSIC CUE #15.)

ACT II

Scene 8

SCENE: *The same. A half-hour later. Dinner is coming to an end in dining-room.*

Amanda, Tom and Jim sitting at table as at end of last scene. Lights dim up in both rooms, and MUSIC CUE #15 *ends.*

AMANDA. (*Laughing, as Jim laughs too.*) You know, Mr. O'Connor, I haven't had such a pleasant evening in a very long time.

JIM. (*Rises.*) Well, Mrs. Wingfield, let me give you a toast. Here's to the old South.

AMANDA. The old South. (*Blackout in both rooms.*)

JIM. Hey, Mr. Light Bulb!

AMANDA. Where was Moses when the lights went out? Do you know the answer to that one, Mr. O'Connor?

JIM. No, ma'am, what's the answer to that one?

AMANDA. Well, I heard one answer, but it wasn't very nice. I thought you might know another one.

JIM. No, ma'am.

AMANDA. It's lucky I put those candles on the table. I just put them on for ornamentation, but it's nice when they prove useful, too.

JIM. Yes, ma'am.

AMANDA. Now, if one of you gentlemen can provide me with a match we can have some illumination.

JIM. (*Lighting candles. Dim in glow for candles.*) I can, ma'am.

AMANDA. Thank you.

JIM. (*Crosses back to R. of dining-room table.*) Not at all, ma'am.

AMANDA. I guess it must be a burnt-out fuse. Mr. O'Connor, do you know anything about a burnt-out fuse?

JIM, I know a little about them, ma'am, but where's the fuse box?

AMANDA. Must you know that, too? Well, it's in the kitchen. (*Jim exits R. into kitchen.*) Be careful. It's dark. Don't stumble over anything. (*Sound of crash off-stage.*) Oh, my goodness, wouldn't it be awful if we lost him! Are you all right, Mr. O'Connor?

JIM. (*Off-stage.*) Yes, ma'am, I'm all right.

AMANDA. You know, electricity is a very mysterious thing. The whole universe is mysterious to me. Wasn't it Benjamin Franklin who tied a key to a kite? I'd like to have seen that—he might have looked mighty silly. Some people say that science clears up all the mysteries for us. In my opinion they just keep on adding more. Haven't you found it yet?

JIM. (*Re-enters R.*) Yes, ma'am. I found it all right, but them fuses look okay to me. (*Sits as before.*)

AMANDA. Tom.

TOM. Yes, Mother?

AMANDA. That light bill I gave you several days ago. The one I got the notice about?

TOM. Oh—yeah. You mean last month's bill?

AMANDA. You didn't neglect it by any chance?

TOM. Well, I ——

AMANDA. You did! I might have known it!

JIM. Oh, maybe Shakespeare wrote a poem on that light bill, Mrs. Wingfield?

AMANDA. Maybe he did, too. I might have known better than to trust him with it! There's such a high price for negligence in this world today.

JIM. Maybe the poem will win a ten-dollar prize.

AMANDA. We'll just have to spend the rest of the evening in the nineteenth century, before Mr. Edison found that Mazda lamp!

JIM. Candle-light is my favorite kind of light.

AMANDA. That shows you're romantic! But that's no excuse for Tom. However, I think it was very nice of them to let us finish our dinner before they plunged us into everlasting darkness. Tom, as a penalty for your carelessness you can help me with the dishes.

JIM. (Rising. Tom rises.) Can I be of some help, ma'am?

AMANDA. (Rising.) Oh, no, I couldn't allow that.

JIM. Well, I ought to be good for *something*.

AMANDA. What did I hear?

JIM. I just said, "I ought to be good for something."

AMANDA. That's what I thought you said. Well, Laura's all by her lonesome out front. Maybe you'd like to keep her company. I can give you this lovely old candelabrum for light. (*Jim takes candles.*) It used to be on the altar at the Church of the Heavenly Rest, but it was melted a little out of shape when the church burnt down. The church was struck by lightning one spring, and Gypsy Jones who was holding a revival meeting in the village, said that the church was struck by lightning because the Episcopalians had started to have card parties right in the church.

JIM. Is that so, ma'am?

AMANDA. I never say anything that isn't so.

JIM. I beg your pardon.

AMANDA. (*Pouring wine into glass—hands it to Jim.*) I'd like Laura to have a little dandelion wine. Do you think you can hold them both?

JIM. I can try, ma'am.

AMANDA. (*Exits U. R. into kitchen.*) Now, Tom, you get into your apron.

TOM. Yes, Mother. (*Follows Amanda. Jim looks around, puts wine-glass down, takes swig from wine decanter, replaces it with thud, takes wine-glass—enters living-room. Inner curtains close as dining-room dims out. Laura sits up nervously as Jim enters. Her speech at first is low and breathless from the almost intolerable strain of being alone with a stranger. In her speeches in this scene, before Jim's warmth overcomes her paralyzing shyness, Laura's voice is thin and breathless as though she has just run up a steep flight of stairs.*)

JIM. (*Entering holding candelabra with lighted candles in one hand and glass of wine in other, and stands.*) How are you feeling now? Any better? (*Jim's attitude is gently humorous. In playing this scene it should be stressed that while the incident is apparently unimportant, it is to Laura the climax of her secret life.*)

LAURA. Yes, thank you.

JIM. (*Gives her glass of wine.*) Oh, here, this is for you. It's a little dandelion wine.

LAURA. Thank you.

JIM. (*Crosses* C.) Well, drink it—but don't get drunk. (*He laughs heartily.*) Say, where'll I put the candles?

LAURA. Oh, anywhere . . .

JIM. Oh, how about right here on the floor? You got any objections?

LAURA. No.

JIM. I'll just spread a newspaper under it to catch the drippings. (*Gets newspaper from armchair. Puts candelabra down on floor* C.) I like to sit on the floor. (*Sits on floor.*) Mind if I do?

LAURA. Oh, no.

JIM. Would you give me a pillow?

LAURA. What?

JIM. A pillow!

LAURA. Oh . . . (*Puts wine-glass on telephone table, hands him pillow, sits* L. *on day-bed.*)

JIM. How about you? Don't you like to sit on the floor?

LAURA. Oh, yes.

JIM. Well, why don't you?

LAURA. I—will.

JIM. Take a pillow! (*Throws pillow as she sits on floor.*) I can't see you sitting way over there. (*Sits on floor again.*)

LAURA. I can—see you.

54

JIM. Yeah, but that's not fair. I'm right here in the limelight. (*Laura moves a little closer to him.*) Good! Now I can see you! Are you comfortable?

LAURA. Yes. Thank you.

JIM. So am I. I'm comfortable as a cow! Say, would you care for a piece of chewing-gum? (*Offers gum.*)

LAURA. No, thank you.

JIM. I think that I will indulge. (*Musingly unwraps it and holds it up.*) Gee, think of the fortune made by the guy that invented the first piece of chewing-gum! It's amazing, huh? Do you know that the Wrigley Building is one of the sights of Chicago?—I saw it summer before last at the Century of Progress.—Did you take in the Century of Progress?

LAURA. No, I didn't.

JIM. Well, it was a wonderful exposition, believe me. You know what impressed me most? The Hall of Science. Gives you an idea of what the future will be like in America. Oh, it's more wonderful than the present time is! Say, your brother tells me you're shy. Is that right, Laura?

LAURA. I—don't know.

JIM. I judge you to be an old-fashioned type of girl. Oh, I think that's a wonderful type to be. I hope you don't think I'm being too personal—do you?

LAURA. Mr. O'Connor?

JIM. Huh?

LAURA. I believe I *will* take a piece of gum, if you don't mind. (*Jim peels gum—gets on knees, hands it to Laura. She breaks off a tiny piece. Jim looks at what remains, puts it in his mouth, and sits again.*) Mr. O'Connor, have you—kept up with your singing?

JIM. Singing? Me?

LAURA. Yes. I remember what a beautiful voice you had.

JIM. You heard me sing?

LAURA. Oh, yes! Very often. . . . I—don't suppose—you remember me—at all?

JIM. (*Smiling doubtfully.*) You know, as a matter of fact I did have an idea I'd seen you before. Do you know it seemed almost like I was about to remember your name. But the name I was about to remember—wasn't a name! So I stopped myself before I said it.

LAURA. Wasn't it—Blue Roses?

JIM. (*Grinning.*) Blue Roses! Oh, my gosh, yes—Blue Roses! You

55

know, I didn't connect you with high school somehow or other. But that's where it was, it was high school. Gosh, I didn't even know you were Shakespeare's sister! Gee, I'm sorry.

LAURA. I didn't expect you to.—You—barely knew me!

JIM. But, we did have a speaking acquaintance.

LAURA. Yes, we—spoke to each other.

JIM. Say, didn't we have a class in something together?

LAURA. Yes, we did.

JIM. What class was that?

LAURA. It was—singing—chorus!

JIM. Aw!

LAURA. I sat across the aisle from you in the auditorium. Mondays, Wednesdays and Fridays.

JIM. Oh, yeah! I remember now—you're the one who always came in late.

LAURA. Yes, it was so hard for me, getting upstairs. I had that brace on my leg then—it clumped so loud!

JIM. I never heard any clumping.

LAURA. (*Wincing at recollection.*) To me it sounded like—thunder!

JIM. I never even noticed.

LAURA. Everybody was seated before I came in. I had to walk in front of all those people. My seat was in the back row. I had to go clumping up the aisle with everyone watching!

JIM. Oh, gee, you shouldn't have been self-conscious.

LAURA. I know, but I was. It was always such a relief when the singing started.

JIM. I remember now. And I used to call you Blue Roses. How did I ever get started calling you a name like that?

LAURA. I was out of school a little while with pleurosis. When I came back you asked me what was the matter. I said I had pleurosis and you thought I said Blue Roses. So that's what you always called me after that!

JIM. I hope you didn't mind?

LAURA. Oh, no—I liked it. You see, I wasn't acquainted with many—people . . .

JIM. Yeah. I remember you sort of stuck by yourself.

LAURA. I never did have much luck at making friends.

JIM. Well, I don't see why you wouldn't.

LAURA. Well, I started out badly.

56

JIM. You mean being ——?

LAURA. Well, yes, it—sort of—stood between me . . .

JIM. You shouldn't have let it!

LAURA. I know, but it did, and I ——

JIM. You mean you were shy with people!

LAURA. I tried not to be but never could ——

JIM. Overcome it?

LAURA. No, I—never could!

JIM. Yeah. I guess being shy is something you have to work out of kind of gradually.

LAURA. Yes—I guess it ——

JIM. Takes time!

LAURA. Yes . . .

JIM. Say, you know something, Laura? (*Rises to sit on day-bed* R.) People are not so dreadful when you know them. That's what you have to remember! And everybody has problems, not just you but practically everybody has problems. You think of yourself as being the only one who is disappointed. But just look around you and what do you see—a lot of people just as disappointed as you are. You take me, for instance. Boy, when I left high school I thought I'd be a lot further along at this time than I am now. Say, you remember that wonderful write-up I had in "The Torch"?

LAURA. Yes, I do! (*She gets year-book from under pillow* L. *of day-bed.*)

JIM. Said I was bound to succeed in anything I went into! Holy Jeez! "The Torch"! (*She opens book, shows it to him and sits next to him on day-bed.*)

LAURA. Here you are in "The Pirates of Penzance"!

JIM. "The Pirates"! "Oh, better far to live and die under the brave black flag I fly!" I sang the lead in that operetta.

LAURA. So beautifully!

JIM. Aw . . .

LAURA. Yes, yes—beautifully—beautifully!

JIM. You heard me then, huh?

LAURA. I heard you all three times!

JIM. No!

LAURA. Yes.

JIM. You mean all three performances?

LAURA. Yes!

JIM. What for?

57

LAURA. I--wanted to ask you to—autograph my program. (*Takes program from book.*)

JIM. Why didn't you ask me?

LAURA. You were always surrounded by your own friends so much that I never had a chance.

JIM. Aw, you should have just come right up and said, Here is my ——

LAURA. Well, I—thought you might think I was ——

JIM. Thought I might think you was—what?

LAURA. Oh ——

JIM. (*With reflective relish.*) Oh! Yeah, I was beleaguered by females in those days.

LAURA. You were terribly popular!

JIM. Yeah . . .

LAURA. You had such a—friendly way ——

JIM. Oh, I was spoiled in high school.

LAURA. Everybody liked you!

JIM. Including you?

LAURA. I—why, yes, I—I did, too. . . .

JIM. Give me that program, Laura. (*She does so, and he signs it.*) There you are—better late than never!

LAURA. My—what a—surprise!

JIM. My signature's not worth very much right now. But maybe some day—it will increase in value! You know, being disappointed is one thing and being discouraged is something else. Well, I may be disappointed but I am not discouraged. Say, you finished high school?

LAURA. I made bad grades in my final examinations.

JIM. You mean you dropped out?

LAURA. (*Rises.*) I didn't go back. (*Crosses* R. *to menagerie. Jim lights cigarette still sitting on day-bed. Laura puts year-book under menagerie. Rises, picks up unicorn—small glass object—her back to Jim. When she touches unicorn. [MUSIC CUE #16-A].*) How is—Emily Meisenbach getting along?

JIM. That kraut-head!

LAURA. Why do you call her that?

JIM. Because that's what she was.

LAURA. You're not still—going with her?

JIM. Oh, I never even see her.

LAURA. It said in the Personal section that you were—engaged!

58

JIM. Uh-huh. I know, but I wasn't impressed by that—propaganda!

LAURA. It wasn't—the truth?

JIM. It was only true in Emily's optimistic opinion!

LAURA. Oh . . . (*Turns* R. *of Jim. Jim lights a cigarette and leans indolently back on his elbows smiling at Laura with a warmth and charm which lights her inwardly with altar candles. She remains by the glass menagerie table and turns in her hands a piece of glass to cover her tumult* CUT MUSIC #16-A.)

JIM. What have you done since high school? Huh?

LAURA. What?

JIM. I said what have you done since high school?

LAURA. Nothing much.

JIM. You must have been doing something all this time.

LAURA. Yes.

JIM. Well, then, such as what?

LAURA. I took a business course at business college . . .

JIM. You did? How did that work out?

LAURA. (*Turns back to Jim.*) Well, not very—well. . . . I had to drop out, it gave me—indigestion. . . .

JIM. (*Laughs gently.*) What are you doing now?

LAURA. I don't do anything—much. . . . Oh, please don't think I sit around doing nothing! My glass collection takes a good deal of time. Glass is something you have to take good care of.

JIM. What did you say—about glass?

LAURA. (*She clears her throat and turns away again, acutely shy.*) Collection, I said—I have one.

JIM. (*Puts out cigarette. Abruptly.*) Say! You know what I judge to be the trouble with you? (*Rises from day-bed and crosses* R.) Inferiority complex! You know what that is? That's what they call it when a fellow low-rates himself! Oh, I understand it because I had it, too. Uh-huh! Only my case was not as aggravated as yours seems to be. I had it until I took up public speaking and developed my voice, and learned that I had an aptitude for science. Do you know that until that time I never thought of myself as being outstanding in any way whatsoever!

LAURA. Oh, my!

JIM. Now I've never made a regular study of it—(*Sits armchair* R.) mind you, but I have a friend who says I can analyze people better than doctors that make a profession of it. I don't claim that's necessarily true, but I can sure guess a person's psychology. Excuse me, Laura. (*Takes out gum.*) I always take it out when the flavor is gone. I'll just wrap it in a piece of paper. (*Tears a piece of paper off the newspaper under candelabrum, wraps gum in it, crosses to day-bed, looks to see if Laura is watching. She isn't. Crosses around day-bed.*) I know how it is when you get it stuck on a shoe. (*Throws gum under day-bed, crosses around L. of day-bed. Crosses R. to Laura.*) Yep—that's what I judge to be your principal trouble. A lack of confidence in yourself as a person. Now I'm basing that fact on a number of your remarks and on certain observations I've made. For instance, that clumping you thought was so awful in high school. You say that you dreaded to go upstairs? You see what you did? You dropped out of school, you gave up an education all because of a little clump, which as far as I can see is practically non-existent! Oh, a little physical defect is all you have. It's hardly noticeable even! Magnified a thousand times by your imagination! You know what my strong advice to you is? You've got to think of yourself as *superior* in some way! (*Crosses L. to small table R. of day-bed. Sits. Laura sits in armchair.*)

LAURA. In what way would I think?

JIM. Why, man alive, Laura! Look around you a little and what do you see? A world full of common people! All of 'em born and all of 'em going to die! Now, which of them has one-tenth of your strong points! Or mine! Or anybody else's for that matter? You see, everybody excels in some one thing. Well—some in many! You take me, for instance. My interest happens to lie in electro-dynamics. I'm taking a course in radio engineering at night school, on top of a fairly responsible job at the warehouse. I'm taking that course *and* studying public speaking.

LAURA. Ohhhh. My!

JIM. Because I believe in the future of television! I want to be ready to go right up along with it. (*Rises, crosses R.*) I'm planning to get in on the ground floor. Oh, I've already made the right connections. All that remains now is for the industry itself to get under way—full steam! You know, *knowledge*—ZSZZppp! *Money*—Zzzzzzpp! *POWER!* Wham! That's the cycle democracy is built on! (*Pause.*) I guess you think I think a lot of myself!

LAURA. No—o-o-o, I don't.

JIM. (*Kneels at armchair R.*) Well, now how about you? Isn't

60

there some one thing that you take more interest in than anything
else?

LAURA. Oh—yes . . .

JIM. Well, then, such as what?

LAURA. Well, I do—as I said—have my—glass collection . . .
(MUSIC CUE #16-A.)

JIM. Oh, you do. What kind of glass is it?

LAURA. (*Takes glass ornament off shelf.*) Little articles of it,
ornaments mostly. Most of them are little animals made out of
glass, the tiniest little animals in the world. Mother calls them the
glass menagerie! Here's an example of one, if you'd like to see it!
This is one of the oldest, it's nearly thirteen. (*Hands it to Jim.*)
Oh, be careful—if you breathe, it breaks! (THE BELL SOLO
SHOULD BEGIN HERE. *This is last part of* CUE #16-A *and
should play to end of record.*)

JIM. I'd better not take it. I'm pretty clumsy with things.

LAURA. Go on, I trust you with him! (*Jim takes horse.*) There
—you're holding him gently! Hold him over the light, he loves the
light! (*Jim holds horse up to light.*) See how the light shines
through him?

JIM. It sure does shine!

LAURA. I shouldn't be partial, but he is my favorite one.

JIM. Say, what kind of a thing is this one supposed to be?

LAURA. Haven't you noticed the single horn on his forehead?

JIM. Oh, a unicorn, huh?

LAURA. Mmmm-hmmmmm!

JIM. Unicorns, aren't they extinct in the modern world?

LAURA. I know!

JIM. Poor little fellow must feel kind of lonesome.

LAURA. Well, if he does he doesn't complain about it. He stays
on a shelf with some horses that don't have horns and they all
seem to get along nicely together.

JIM. They do. Say, where will I put him?

LAURA. Put him on the table. (*Jim crosses to small table* R. *of
day-bed, puts unicorn on it.*) They all like a change of scenery
once in a while!

JIM. (C., *facing upstage, stretching arms.*) They do. (MUSIC
CUE #16-B: *Dance Music.*) Hey! Look how big my shadow is
when I stretch.

61

LAURA. (*Crossing to* L. *of day-bed.*) Oh, oh, yes—it stretched across the ceiling!

JIM. (*Crosses to door* R., *exits, leaving door open, and stands on fire-escape landing. Sings to music. [Popular record of day for dance-hall.] When Jim opens door, music swells.*) It's stopped raining. Where does the music come from?

LAURA. From the Paradise Dance Hall across the alley.

JIM. (*Re-entering room, closing door* R., *crosses to Laura.*) How about cutting the rug a little, Miss Wingfield? Or is your program filled up? Let me take a look at it. (*Crosses back* C. *Music, in dance hall, goes into a waltz. Business here with imaginary dance-program card.*) Oh, say! Every dance is taken! I'll just scratch some of them out. Ahhhh, a waltz! (*Crosses to Laura.*)

LAURA. I—can't dance!

JIM. There you go with that inferiority stuff!

LAURA. I've never danced in my life!

JIM. Come on, try!

LAURA. Oh, but I'd step on you!

JIM. Well, I'm not made out of glass.

LAURA. How—how do we start?

JIM. You hold your arms out a little.

LAURA. Like this?

JIM. A little bit higher. (*Takes Laura in arms.*) That's right. Now don't tighten up, that's the principal thing about it—just relax.

LAURA. It's hard not to.

JIM. Okay.

LAURA. I'm afraid you can't budge me.

JIM. (*Dances around* L. *of day-bed slowly.*) What do you bet I can't?

LAURA. Goodness, yes, you can!

JIM. Let yourself go, now, Laura, just let yourself go.

LAURA. I'm ——

JIM. Come on!

LAURA. Trying!

JIM. Not so stiff now—easy does it!

LAURA. I know, but I'm ——!

JIM. Come on! Loosen your backbone a little! (*When they get to up-stage corner of day-bed—so that the audience will not see him lift her—Jim's arm tightens around her waist and he swings her around* C. *with her feet off floor about 3 complete turns before they hit the small table* R. *of day-bed. Music swells as Jim lifts her.*) There we go! (*Jim knocks glass horse off table.* MUSIC FADES.)

LAURA. Oh, it doesn't matter ——

JIM. (*Picks horse up.*) We knocked the little glass horse over.

LAURA. Yes.

JIM. (*Hands unicorn to Laura.*) Is he broken?

LAURA. Now he's just like all the other horses.

JIM. You mean he lost his ——?

LAURA. He's lost his horn. It doesn't matter. Maybe it's a blessing in disguise.

JIM. Gee, I bet you'll never forgive me. I bet that was your favorite piece of glass.

LAURA. Oh, I don't have favorites—(*Pause.*) much. It's no tragedy. Glass breaks so easily. No matter how careful you are. The traffic jars the shelves and things fall off them.

JIM. Still I'm awfully sorry that I was the cause of it.

LAURA. I'll just imagine he had an operation. The horn was removed to make him feel less—freakish! (*Crosses* L., *sits on small table.*) Now he will feel more at home with the other horses, the ones who don't have horns. . . .

JIM. (*Sits on arm of armchair* R., *faces Laura.*) I'm glad to see that you have a sense of humor. You know—you're—different than anybody else I know? (MUSIC CUE #17.) Do you mind me telling you that? I mean it. You make me feel sort of—I don't know how to say it! I'm usually pretty good at expressing things, but—this is something I don't know how to say! Did anybody ever tell you that you were pretty? (*Rises, crosses to Laura.*) Well, you are! And in a different way from anyone else. And all the nicer because of the difference. Oh, boy, I wish that you were my sister. I'd teach you to have confidence in yourself. Being different is nothing to be ashamed of. Because other people aren't such wonderful people. They're a hundred times one thousand. You're one times one! They walk all over the earth. You just stay here. They're as common as—weeds, but—you, well you're—*Blue Roses!*

LAURA. But blue is—wrong for—roses . . .

JIM. It's right for you!—You're pretty!

LAURA. In what respect am I pretty?

JIM. In all respects—your eyes—your hair. Your hands are pretty! You think I'm saying this because I'm invited to dinner and have

63

to be nice. Oh, I could do that! I could say lots of things without being sincere. But I'm talking to you sincerely. I happened to notice you had this inferiority complex that keeps you from feeling comfortable with people. Somebody ought to build your confidence up—way up! and make you proud instead of shy and turning away and—blushing —— (*Jim lifts Laura up on small table on "way up."*) Somebody—ought to—(*Lifts her down.*) somebody ought to—kiss you, Laura! (*They kiss. Jim releases her and turns slowly away, crossing a little D. R. Then, quietly, to himself: As Jim turns away, MUSIC ENDS.*) Gee, I shouldn't have done that—that was way off the beam. (*Gives way D. R. Turns to Laura. Laura sits on small table.*) Would you care for a cigarette? You don't smoke, do you? How about a mint? Peppermint—Life-Saver? My pocket's a regular drug-store. . . . Laura, you know, if I had a sister like you, I'd do the same thing as Tom. I'd bring fellows home to meet you. Maybe I shouldn't be saying this. That may not have been the idea in having me over. But what if it was? There's nothing wrong with that.—The only trouble is that in my case—I'm not in a position to —— I can't ask for your number and say I'll phone. I can't call up next week end—ask for a date. I thought I had better explain the situation in case you—misunderstood and I hurt your feelings . . .

LAURA. (*Faintly.*) You—won't—call again?

JIM. (*Crossing to R. of day-bed, and sitting.*) No, I can't. You see, I've—got strings on me. Laura, I've—been going steady! I go out all the time with a girl named Betty. Oh, she's a nice quiet home girl like you, and Catholic and Irish, and in a great many ways we—get along fine. I met her last summer on a moonlight boat trip up the river to Alton, on the *Majestic*. Well—right away from the start it was—love! Oh, boy, being in love has made a new man of me! The power of love is pretty tremendous! Love is something that—changes the whole world. It happened that Betty's aunt took sick and she got a wire and had to go to Centralia. So naturally when Tom asked me to dinner—naturally I accepted the invitation, not knowing—I mean—not knowing. I wish that you would—say something. (*Laura gives Jim unicorn.*) What are you doing that for? You mean you want me to have him? What for?

LAURA. A—souvenir. (*She crosses R. to menagerie. Jim rises.*)

AMANDA. (*Off-stage.*) I'm coming, children. (*She enters into dining-room from kitchen R.*) I thought you'd like some liquid refreshment. (*Puts tray on small table. Lifts a glass.*) Mr. O'Connor, have you heard that song about lemonade? It's

"Lemonade, lemonade,
Made in the shade and stirred with a spade—
And then it's good enough for any old maid!"

JIM. No, ma'am, I never heard it.

AMANDA. Why are you so serious, honey? (*To Laura.*)

JIM. Well, we were having a serious conversation.

AMANDA. I don't understand modern young people. When I was a girl I was gay about everything.

JIM. You haven't changed a bit, Mrs. Wingfield.

AMANDA. I suppose it's the gaiety of the occasion that has rejuvenated me. Well, here's to the gaiety of the occasion! (*Spills lemonade on dress.*) Oooo! I baptized myself. (*Puts glass on small table R. of day-bed.*) I found some cherries in the kitchen, and I put one in each glass.

JIM. You shouldn't gave gone to all that trouble, ma'am.

AMANDA. It was no trouble at all. Didn't you hear us cutting up in the kitchen? I was so outdone with Tom for not bringing you over sooner, but now you've found your way I want you to come all the time—not just once in a while—but all the time. Oh, I think I'll go back in that kitchen. (*Starts to exit* U. C.)

JIM. Oh, no, ma'am, please don't go, ma'am. As a matter of fact, I've got to be going.

AMANDA. Oh, Mr. O'Connor, it's only the shank of the evening! (*Jim and Amanda stand* U. C.)

JIM. Well, you know how it is.

AMANDA. You mean you're a young working man and have to keep workingmen's hours?

JIM. Yes, ma'am.

AMANDA. Well, we'll let you off early this time, but only on the condition that you stay later next time, much later —— What's the best night for you? Saturday?

JIM. Well, as a matter of fact, I have a couple of time-clocks to punch, Mrs. Wingfield, one in the morning and another one at night!

AMANDA. Oh, isn't that nice, you're so ambitious! You work at night, too?

JIM. No, ma'am, not work but—Betty!

AMANDA. (*Crosses* L. *below day-bed.*) Betty? Who's Betty?

JIM. Oh, just a girl. The girl I go steady with!

AMANDA. You mean it's serious? (*Crosses* D. L.)

JIM. Oh, yes, ma'am. We're going to be married the second Sunday in June.

AMANDA. (*Sits on day-bed.*) Tom didn't say anything at all about your going to be married?

JIM. Well, the cat's not out of the bag at the warehouse yet. (*Picks up hat from telephone table.*) You know how they are. They call you Romeo and stuff like that.—It's been a wonderful evening, Mrs. Wingfield. I guess this is what they mean by Southern hospitality.

AMANDA. It was nothing. Nothing at all.

JIM. I hope it don't seem like I'm rushing off. But I promised Betty I'd pick her up at the Wabash depot an' by the time I get my jalopy down there her train'll be in. Some women are pretty upset if you keep them waiting.

AMANDA. Yes, I know all about the tyranny of women! Well, good-bye, Mr. O'Connor. (*Amanda puts out hand. Jim takes it.*) I wish you happiness—and good fortune. You wish him that, too, don't you, Laura?

LAURA. Yes, I do, Mother.

JIM. (*Crosses* L. *to Laura.*) Good-bye, Laura. I'll always treasure that souvenir. And don't you forget the good advice I gave you. So long, Shakespeare! (*Up* C.) Thanks, again, ladies.—Good night! (*He grins and ducks jauntily out* R.)

AMANDA. (*Faintly.*) Well, well, well. Things have a way of turning out so badly —— (*Laura crosses to phonograph, puts on record.*) I don't believe that I would play the victrola. Well, well —well, our gentleman caller was engaged to be married! Tom!

TOM. (*Off.*) Yes, Mother?

AMANDA. Come out here. I want to tell you something very funny.

TOM. (*Entering through* R. *kitchen door to dining-room and into living-room, through curtains,* D. C.) Has the gentleman caller gotten away already?

AMANDA. The gentleman caller made a very early departure. That was a nice joke you played on us, too!

TOM. How do you mean?

AMANDA. You didn't mention that he was engaged to be married.

TOM. Jim? Engaged?

66

AMANDA. That's what he just informed us.

TOM. I'll be jiggered! I didn't know.

AMANDA. That seems very peculiar.

TOM. What's peculiar about it?

AMANDA. Didn't you tell me he was your best friend down at the warehouse?

TOM. He is, but how did I know?

AMANDA. It seems very peculiar you didn't know your best friend was engaged to be married!

TOM. The warehouse is the place where I work, not where I know things about people!

AMANDA. You don't know things anywhere! You live in a dream; you manufacture illusions! (*Tom starts for* R. *door.*) Where are you going? Where are you going? Where are you going?

TOM. I'm going to the movies.

AMANDA. (*Rises, crosses up to Tom.*) That's right, now that you've had us make such fools of ourselves. The effort, the preparations, all the expense! The new floor lamp, the rug, the clothes for Laura! All for what? To entertain some other girl's fiancé! Go to the movies, go! Don't think about us, a mother deserted, an unmarried sister who's crippled and has no job! Don't let anything interfere with your selfish pleasure! Just go, go, go—to the movies!

TOM. All right, I will, and the more you shout at me about my selfish pleasures, the quicker I'll go, and I won't go to the movies either. (*Gets hat from phone table, slams door* R., *and exits up alley* R.)

AMANDA. (*Crosses up to fire-escape landing, yelling.*) Go, then! Then go to the moon—you selfish dreamer! (MUSIC CUE #18. INTERIOR LIGHT *dims out. Re-enters living-room, slamming* R. *door. Tom's closing speech is timed with the interior pantomime. The interior scene is played as though viewed through soundproof glass, behind outer scrim curtain. Amanda, standing, appears to be making a comforting speech to Laura who is huddled on* R. *side of day-bed. Now that we cannot hear the mother's speech, her silliness is gone and she has dignity and tragic beauty. Laura's hair hides her face until at the end of the speech she lifts it to smile at her mother. Amanda's gestures are slow and graceful, almost dance-like, as she comforts her daughter. Tom, who has meantime put on, as before, the jacket and cap, enters down* R. *from off-*

67

stage, and again comes to fire-escape landing, stands as he speaks. Meantime lights are upon Amanda and Laura, but are dim.)

TOM. I didn't go to the moon. I went much farther. For time is the longest distance between two places. . . . I left Saint Louis. I descended these steps of this fire-escape for the last time and followed, from then on, in my father's footsteps, attempting to find in motion what was lost in space. . . . I travelled around a great deal. The cities swept about me like dead leaves, leaves that were brightly colored but torn away from the branches. I would have stopped, but I was pursued by something. It always came upon me unawares, taking me altogether by surprise. Perhaps it was a familiar bit of music. Perhaps it was only a piece of transparent glass. . . . Perhaps I am walking along a street at night, in some strange city, before I have found companions, and I pass the lighted window of a shop where perfume is sold. The window is filled with pieces of colored glass, tiny transparent bottles in delicate colors, like bits of a shattered rainbow. Then all at once my sister touches my shoulder. I turn around and look into her eyes. . . . Oh, Laura, Laura, I tried to leave you behind me, but I am more faithful than I intended to be! I reach for a cigarette, I cross the street, I run into a movie or a bar. I buy a drink, I speak to the nearest stranger—anything that can blow your candles out!—for nowadays the world is lit by lightning! Blow out your candles, Laura . . . *(Laura blows out candles still burning in candelabrum and the whole interior is blacked out.)* And so— good-bye! *(Exits up alley R. Music continues to the end.)*

CURTAIN
(End of play.)

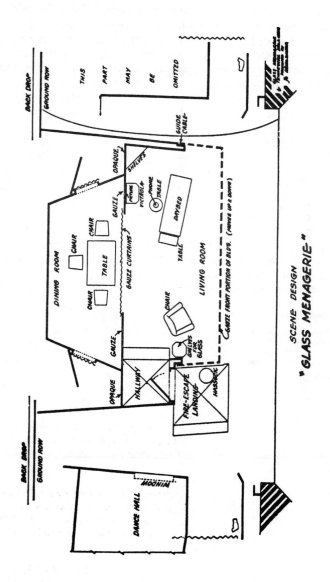

SCENE DESIGN
"GLASS MENAGERIE"

69

PROP LIST

Glass Swan and unicorn, and other glass ornaments
Yearbook (program in book)
Cigarette and matches
Folded newspaper
Typewriter and table; chair; charts
3 dinner plates—forks—bread—beans
Ash-tray
Alarm clock
Rattle, muffler and scarf
2 pillows for couch
2 powder puffs
Vase
Telephone
Lace table-cloth, 3 dinner plates, 4 sets silverware, candelabra, decanter (colored water), 2 wine glasses, silver coffee pot and sugar and creamer, 4 cups and saucers
Newspaper
Jonquils
Chewing-gum
Pencil
Life-savers (mints)

TODAY'S HOTTEST NEW PLAYS

❑ **MOLLY SWEENEY by Brian Friel, Tony Award-Winning Author of** *Dancing at Lughnasa.* Told in the form of monologues by three related characters, *Molly Sweeney* is mellifluous, Irish storytelling at its dramatic best. Blind since birth, Molly recounts the effects of an eye operation that was intended to restore her sight but which has unexpected and tragic consequences. *"Brian Friel has been recognized as Ireland's greatest living playwright. Molly Sweeney confirms that Mr. Friel still writes like a dream. Rich with rapturous poetry and the music of rising and falling emotions...Rarely has Mr. Friel written with such intoxicating specificity about scents, colors and contours."* - New York Times. [2M, 1W]

❑ **SWINGING ON A STAR (The Johnny Burke Musical) by Michael Leeds. 1996 Tony Award Nominee for Best Musical.** The fabulous songs of Johnny Burke are perfectly represented here in a series of scenes jumping from a 1920s Chicago speakeasy to a World War II USO Show and on through the romantic high jinks of the Bob Hope/Bing Crosby "Road Movies." Musical numbers include such favorites as "Pennies from Heaven," "Misty," "Ain't It a Shame About Mame," "Like Someone in Love," and, of course, the Academy Award winning title song, "Swinging on a Star." *"A WINNER. YOU'LL HAVE A BALL!"* - New York Post. *"A dazzling, toe-tapping, finger-snapping delight!"* - ABC Radio Network. *"Johnny Burke wrote his songs with moonbeams!"* - New York Times. [3M, 4W]

❑ **THE MONOGAMIST by Christopher Kyle.** Infidelity and mid-life anxiety force a forty-something poet to reevaluate his 60s values in a late 80s world. *"THE BEST COMEDY OF THE SEASON. Trenchant, dark and jagged. Newcomer Christopher Kyle is a playwright whose social satire comes with a nasty, ripping edge - Molière by way of Joe Orton."* - Variety. *"By far the most stimulating playwright I've encountered in many a buffaloed moon."* - New York Magazine. *"Smart, funny, articulate and wisely touched with rue...the script radiates a bright, bold energy."* - The Village Voice. [2M, 3W]

❑ **DURANG/DURANG by Christopher Durang.** These cutting parodies of *The Glass Menagerie* and *A Lie of the Mind*, along with the other short plays in the collection, prove once and for all that Christopher Durang is our theater's unequivocal master of outrageous comedy. *"The fine art of parody has returned to theater in a production you can sink your teeth and mind into, while also laughing like an idiot."* - New York Times. *"If you need a break from serious drama, the place to go is Christopher Durang's silly, funny, over-the-top sketches."* - TheatreWeek. [3M, 4W, flexible casting]

DRAMATISTS PLAY SERVICE, INC.
440 Park Avenue South, New York, New York 10016 212-683-8960 Fax 212-213-1539

TODAY'S HOTTEST NEW PLAYS

❑ **THREE VIEWINGS by Jeffrey Hatcher.** Three comic-dramatic monologues, set in a midwestern funeral parlor, interweave as they explore the ways we grieve, remember, and move on. *"Finally, what we have been waiting for: a new, true, idiosyncratic voice in the theater. And don't tell me you hate monologues; you can't hate them more than I do. But these are much more: windows into the deep of each speaker's fascinating, paradoxical, unique soul, and windows out into a gallery of surrounding people, into hilarious and horrific coincidences and conjunctions, into the whole dirty but irresistible business of living in this damnable but spellbinding place we presume to call the world."* - New York Magazine. [1M, 2W]

❑ **HAVING OUR SAY by Emily Mann.** The Delany Sisters' Bestselling Memoir is now one of Broadway's Best-Loved Plays! Having lived over one hundred years apiece, Bessie and Sadie Delany have plenty to say, and their story is not simply African-American history or women's history...it is our history as a nation. *"The most provocative and entertaining family play to reach Broadway in a long time."* - New York Times. *"Fascinating, marvelous, moving and forceful."* - Associated Press. [2W]

❑ **THE YOUNG MAN FROM ATLANTA Winner of the 1995 Pulitzer Prize. by Horton Foote.** An older couple attempts to recover from the suicide death of their only son, but the menacing truth of why he died, and what a certain Young Man from Atlanta had to do with it, keeps them from the peace they so desperately need. *"Foote ladles on character and period nuances with a density unparalleled in any living playwright."* - NY Newsday. [5M, 4W]

❑ **SIMPATICO by Sam Shepard.** Years ago, two men organized a horse racing scam. Now, years later, the plot backfires against the ringleader when his partner decides to come out of hiding. *"Mr. Shepard writing at his distinctive, savage best."* - New York Times. [3M, 3W]

❑ **MOONLIGHT by Harold Pinter.** The love-hate relationship between a dying man and his family is the subject of Harold Pinter's first full-length play since *Betrayal*. *"Pinter works the language as a master pianist works the keyboard."* - New York Post. [4M, 2W, 1G]

❑ **SYLVIA by A.R. Gurney.** This romantic comedy, the funniest to come along in years, tells the story of a twenty-two year old marriage on the rocks, and of Sylvia, the dog who turns it all around. *"A delicious and dizzy new comedy."* - New York Times. *"FETCHING! I hope it runs longer than Cats!"* - New York Daily News. [2M, 2W]

DRAMATISTS PLAY SERVICE, INC.

440 Park Avenue South, New York, New York 10016 212-683-8960 Fax 212-213-1539